MINUTE BY MINUTE...

RANDOM HOUSE
NEW YORK

MINUTE BY MINUTE...

DON HEWITT

PHOTO CREDITS:
PAGE 16: THE BETTMANN ARCHIVE; PAGE 171: CBS (LEFT), MIKE FULLER (RIGHT).
PAGE 172: MAGGIE O'BRYAN/CBS NEWS (LEFT), CBS (RIGHT); PAGE 173: MAGGIE O'BRYAN/CBS NEWS (BOTH).
PAGE 174: MAGGIE O'BRYAN/CBS NEWS (BOTH); PAGE 175: MAGGIE O'BRYAN/CBS NEWS (BOTH).
ALL OTHER PHOTOGRAPHS COURTESY OF CBS NEWS.

PUBLISHED IN THE UNITED STATES BY RANDOM HOUSE, INC., NEW YORK, AND
SIMULTANEOUSLY IN CANADA BY RANDOM HOUSE OF CANADA LIMITED, TORONTO.

LIBRARY OF CONGRESS CATALOGING IN PUBLICATION DATA
HEWITT, DON, 1922–
MINUTE BY MINUTE.

1. 60 MINUTES (TELEVISION PROGRAM) 2. TELEVISION
BROADCASTING OF NEWS—UNITED STATES. 3. HEWITT, DON,
1922– 4. TELEVISION PRODUCERS AND DIRECTORS—
UNITED STATES—BIOGRAPHY. I. TITLE.
PN4888.T4H48 1985 791.45'72 85-10718

ISBN 0-394-54641-5

98765432

FIRST EDITION

MANUFACTURED IN THE UNITED STATES OF AMERICA

FOR WILLIAM S. PALEY

AND MY WIFE, MARILYN

TWO PEOPLE I LOVE

CONTENTS

AUTHOR'S NOTE

If you wonder, as I do, when so much of a book is in quotes, if the author always had a notebook and tape recorder with him—this author didn't. What this author had with him was pretty good recall, and to the best of his recollection what's in quotes is what was said or what he was told was said. The author cannot swear that all the quotes are verbatim, but he can swear that they're close enough not to be distorted, dishonest or disingenuous.

As for the transcripts from *60 Minutes*. Included in this book are some of the more delicious moments from the show. But the transcripts and still photographs cannot capture the shrugs, the grins, the grimaces that punctuate great moments on television. So some of the transcripts have been edited slightly—very slightly—to help convey to a reader the same impressions that were conveyed to the viewer.

PROLOGUE

Thirty-seven years is a long time to work for anyone, but in television thirty-seven years with the same company is almost unheard of. Everybody is always moving. If they're not going from CBS to ABC, they're going from ABC to NBC or vice versa. Sometimes they even go around the circuit two or three times, but by the time they get to be my age they've usually gone down the drain. I'm still here mostly because they think that without me *60 Minutes* would go down the drain. I'm not sure I buy that, but I'm glad *they* do.

Trying to keep up with the eighties when you were born in the twenties is not as much of a chore as you might think. In some ways it helps not to be of the age you are reporting on and to stand back occasionally and take it in like a visitor from another planet. For instance, nobody shouts "Extra!" anymore. What they say is, "We interrupt this program . . ."; but every time they say that what I hear is "Extra!"

In my head there is only one movie and it is called *Gone With the Wind*. There is only one President and his name is Franklin Roosevelt. I know it's not true that "they don't make them like that anymore," but isn't it true that they haven't made any Bill Paleys or Fiorello La Guardias in a long time? I know that several people have broken the four-minute mile but it's tough to convince me that anybody has run a mile faster than Glenn Cunningham did when he ran 4:04:04 in 1938 or that anyone has jumped farther than Jesse Owens did in the 1936 Olympics or can play a clarinet better than Benny Goodman or sing better than Billie Holiday or write better than Ernest Hemingway. It's tough to find a "legend" these days, someone who marks for us a whole era and not just individual years. Television is, I think, the culprit. Television, which has been so good to me, has been so bad for "legends." We eat 'em up and spit 'em out before they can become legends, and it's tough to know where a Michael Jackson or a Reggie Jackson or a Jesse Jackson fits in.

I like it that I can get to London in six and a half hours (three and a half on the Concorde), but I liked it better when it took twelve with a stop in Gander or Goose Bay or Shannon or the Azores. You had the feeling then that you were really going somewhere and that London or Paris or Rome wasn't just around the corner. I also liked it better when it took four years to get from twelve to sixteen, and growing up wasn't just around the corner.

When I was growing up in New Rochelle, New York, it wasn't the heartland of America, but with very little trouble you could forget that it was only forty-five minutes from Broadway. It had 60,000 people and it seemed that all 60,000 knew one another. Along with most of the other people in town, we were just barely middle class. If a strong wind had come up, it would have blown us back into the lower class. I wasn't exactly Tom Sawyer or Huck Finn, but I built a raft and sailed it on a pond in the north end of town and fished with worms and necked in parked cars and cut school to go hear Tommy Dorsey at the Paramount. It didn't seem to be a big deal to the boys I fished with or the girls I necked with that I was Jewish, and it didn't seem to me to be a big deal either. It just was. I stayed home from school on Rosh Hashanah and Yom Kippur and went to my grandfather's for Passover, but I also got Christmas presents and ran on the track team of the Catholic Youth Organization and went to dances at the North Avenue Presbyterian Church. Yom Kippur, Easter, Rosh Hashanah, Christmas were all my holidays.

Have I stopped being Jewish? Good God no! I am probably more Jewish by temperament than most of the Jews I know. It's just that to me it's never been a big deal.

Being white hasn't been a big deal either. In the years since I grew up, I've had three heroes. Two of them, Martin Luther King and Willie Mays, were black, and one of them, Bobby Kennedy, was white.

My father, who sold advertising for Hearst Newspapers, had two particular heroes, Joe Louis and Eleanor Roosevelt. When Joe Louis knocked out Max Schmeling my father let out a whoop and did a little dance in front of the radio, and when Westbrook Pegler beat up on Mrs. Roosevelt he fumed. In our crowd that seemed to be the measure of how liberal you were—how much you liked Mrs. Roosevelt and how hard you rooted for Joe Louis. That's about as far as it went. The people who went farther were called "commies" and nobody wanted to be called one of *those,* so we never got very much involved in social issues. I think it was because we were chicken and not because we didn't know better.

I also knew better than to taunt the Chinese laundryman next door to the stationery store, but I did. All the kids did. He had an extra finger and was known to us as "the six-fingered Chinaman." One day, one of the kids told us his uncle had told him that the worst thing you could say to a "Chinaman" was "Icka micka heilo eesum gooleay," and we believed it. We used to stand outside on the sidewalk and watch the inscrutable Oriental bent over his ironing board, and if the coast was clear, we would holler "Icka micka heilo eesum gooleay" and run around the corner and hide. I'm sure he thought we were nuts or, at the very least, inscrutable.

When I wasn't taunting the laundryman or doing some other unproductive thing, I sold magazines—*Liberty, Collier's* and the *Woman's Home Companion*—and made enough money to go to the movies every Saturday on the trolley and have enough left over for a frozen Milky Way. With very little effort you could spend most of a Saturday in the movies. There was a Tom Mix, a Tarzan, a cartoon and two full-length pictures.

It was the people up on that screen who became our heroes, but it wasn't Tom Mix or Tarzan who became mine. When I walked out of that movie house I was either Julian Marsh, the Broadway producer in *42nd Street,* or Hildy Johnson, the anything-for-a-story reporter in *The Front Page.*

My problem was that I couldn't decide which one I wanted to be, but lo and behold and abracadabra, fifteen years later along came television, and I could be both of them.

CBS WHATA VISION?

So much of me is in *60 Minutes* and so much of *60 Minutes* is in me that it's hard to write about one without writing about the other.

When I got a job as a copy boy at the now defunct New York *Herald Tribune* in 1942, I thought I had died and gone to heaven or at the very least had gone to sleep and awakened on a movie set. The people who worked there all looked as if they had come from central casting. God, how I loved that place. The job paid $15 a week and the take-home was $14.85 (they took out 15 cents for Social Security). I think it was the best job I ever had.

I arrived at work at four and left at midnight, and our lunch hour came right after the first edition was locked up. It also came at the time the chorus girls at the National Theater next door were changing for the second act, and if you went into an alleyway outside the press room, you could look in their dressing-room window, which was below street level. One night, a sandwich in one hand and a soda pop bottle in the other, I was peering in the window (no wonder I thought I had died and gone to heaven), when I got too close and fell into the ten-foot-deep window well. As I lay there in the darkness I could hear the girls shouting that there was a prowler in the alley, and all I could see was a headline on my hometown newspaper: FORMER CAPTAIN OF HIGH SCHOOL TRACK TEAM ARRESTED AS PEEPING TOM. When I managed to discover a ladder and scramble out of there, dirty and disheveled, I found a phone in the press room and told the city desk that I had suddenly gotten sick and had to go home. I told my parents I had been hit by a taxi, but he got away before I could get his number.

The nights when we copy boys didn't spend our lunch hours peeping at the chorus girls, we went to a bar named Artists and Writers on Fortieth Street (everybody called it Bleeck's)—the same bar where Spencer Tracy and Katharine Hepburn did their drinking in the movie *Woman of the Year*. If I was lucky, someone would buy me a beer. After all, I was only making $15 a week and some of those reporters were already up to $75.

Consequently it was no big financial loss for me when, with the draft board breathing down my neck, I enrolled in the Merchant Marine Academy, a sort of poor man's Annapolis. So how, then, did I, at the age of twenty, become a war correspondent, the youngest one assigned to Eisenhower's headquarters? In the course of a training cruise in the North Atlantic I ended up in London, where I went around to *Stars and Stripes*, the Army newspaper, to see some of the people I had known at the *Trib*. The major in charge decided that a merchant marine correspondent was what the paper lacked and that I was the guy for the job.

In England, waiting for D-Day, I fell in love with just about every Englishman I met . . . whether it was the RAF pilots with whom I flew antisubmarine patrols from Ireland to Iceland or the British sailors with whom I sailed on Hunt-class destroyers looking for German E Boats in the North Sea or the sea captains I wrote about who skippered the rescue ships that fished survivors out of the waters the allied convoys plied on the run to Murmansk. I look for them every time I go back to London, but they're gone and the world will never, I fear, see their like again.

The Brits had marvelous handlebar mustaches, and chests full of ribbons. The Yanks had American cigarettes and nylon stockings. When it came to girls, it really wasn't a fair fight. That's principally why Anglo-American relations in London in 1943 were in such a serious state of disrepair. So the brass—ours and theirs—decided to put on a show. What they decided to do was to have an American general decorate six British sailors and have a British admiral decorate six American soldiers. There, in a mansion in London's Park Lane, under crossed British and American flags, the admiral and his staff and the general and his staff gathered to hand out the medals in front of the combined British and American press.

As the American general shook hands with the British admiral to start the festivities, the photographers hollered "Hold it!," which they did. They all got their shots except for a G.I. cameraman from the U.S. Army Pictorial Service. He kept clicking away but nothing happened. Finally, the American general, realizing that the G.I. was holding up this important display of British-American friendship, said, "What's the matter, son? Something wrong with your camera?" "No, sir," the G.I. replied. "It's these damned Limey bulbs!"

That broke the tension. The British contingent burst out laughing, realizing what a silly exercise they were involved in. We all went back to the pubs, the Limeys and the Yanks, and continued to fight—over girls.

After the war was over, still wearing my war correspondent's uniform, I went back to the New York *Herald Tribune* to be assigned, I was sure, to the foreign staff. I got a big greeting and a lot of pats on the back and was told that of course there was a place for me. I had earned it. Anytime I was ready to take off that war correspondent's uniform I could come back to work—as head copy boy.

So it was a pretty deflated twenty-three-year-old who went around to the Associated Press looking for a job. They had one. It wasn't much but it sure as hell beat being a copy boy, even a head one, and I went to Memphis for about a year. But Mem-

MUSTY OLD ACME

phis was not where it was happening so I quit and went to Pelham, New York, to edit the Pelham *Sun*.

Pelham was a lot closer to New York than Memphis was, but not much happened there either, and six months or so after I arrived I left to work for Acme Newspictures, then the picture arm of the United Press. Acme had a floor in a nondescript office building on Manhattan's Eighth Avenue a block or two below the garment district, and what I did was select pictures shot by Acme photographers, write captions for them and then transmit them by wire to newspaper offices all over the country. Sounds fascinating. It wasn't. The place was musty, and so was the job, and if this was journalism, I thought, maybe I'd better start looking for something more exciting.

One day it came, out of the blue. Bob Rogow, who had worked with me at the *Trib,* was now working for CBS Radio and had heard about an opening at CBS for someone with picture experience.

"What does radio want with someone with picture experience?" I asked him.

"Not radio," he said. "Television."

"*Whata*-vision?" I asked.

"Television!" he said.

"You mean, where you sit at home and watch little pictures in a box?" I asked.

"That's it," he replied. "They got it. I saw it."

"The hell you did."

"The hell I didn't."

"Where did you see it?" I asked.

"Upstairs over Grand Central."

So I went down to Grand Central Station and damned if they didn't have it, up on the top floor—little pictures in a box. They also had cameras and lights and makeup artists and stage managers and microphone booms just like in the movies, and I was hooked. I had been passing through Grand Central every day on my way to work

THE EMERALD CITY

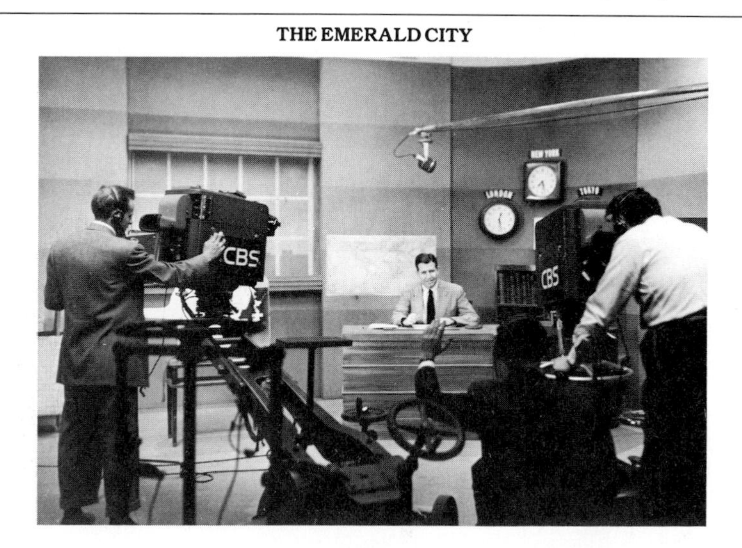

at Acme and never knew that upstairs over the trains and the waiting room and the information booth was an attic stuffed with the most fabulous toys anyone ever had to play with. I wandered around like Judy Garland in the Emerald City gaping at the sets and the control room and finally found the news director, Bob Bendick, who hired me on the spot. I wanted to kiss him.

The next day I told Boyd Lewis, my boss at Acme, that I was leaving.

"For what?" he asked.

"For television," I said proudly.

"Television?" he said. "Television is a fad. It won't last." Boyd was half right. It was a fad, but it lasted.

By the early 1950s I was playing a hot hand. I was producing and directing CBS's five-nights-a-week, fifteen-minute newscast called *Douglas Edwards with the News* and doubling as the producer-director of the big events that we covered live. (It was long before videotape and color, so what came into your living room in those days was in living black and white.)

Back then, most of the jobs in TV didn't pay a whole hell of a lot, so there wasn't a whole hell of a lot of talent around to compete with. I don't mean that there wasn't any talent around. There was Doug Edwards, who was a superb broadcaster. There was a young writer from North Carolina named Charles Kuralt and a charmer from Iowa named Harry Reasoner, who was a natural. There was Alice Weel, who came over from radio a year or two before it was either fashionable or profitable to do that. But nobody else stood out.

The real talent at CBS-TV in those days was a bunch of young directors who wandered over from Broadway to look us over. But they had no interest in news—they directed the big dramatic and variety shows—and in any case they didn't stick around very long. Among them was a fellow named Brynner who left to become a king, and a guy named Lumet who seemed to know even then that Hollywood was waiting for him. The only one of the group who got involved in my end of the business was Frank Schaffner, with whom I shared the directing duties on *Douglas Edwards with the News,* but he also left. Directing George C. Scott in *Patton* and Steve McQueen in *Papillon* was more to Frank's liking than directing *Douglas Edwards with the News,* and besides, it paid better.

Actually, the gang that would eventually make the move from radio still looked down on television. I think they had the feeling, like my boss at Acme, that those little pictures in a box were a fad. But as they and everybody else found out, when you put sound with those little pictures and the show is *60 Minutes,* this is what you get:

MR. & MRS. RICHARD BURTON
March 24, 1970

ELIZABETH TAYLOR:
Fighting is one of the greatest exercises in marital togetherness.

BURTON:
[But] you do not attack the weak parts. . .

TAYLOR:
You bloody well have.

BURTON:
She's got a slightly fat belly. . .

TAYLOR:
. . . your pockmarks, you know.

BURTON:
We can attack these things but they're superficial.

TAYLOR:
No, there are ethics in fighting.

PUCCI:
The word sexy is an Anglo-Saxon word. We use "feminine" . . . This modern concept of sexiness is something completely foreign to our mind . . . The fact of exposing a breast or a behind doesn't seem to be a very important thing to a Latin who has always been surrounded by a pagan conception of life, where breasts and behinds were of very little importance.

ASHE:
One day, I think not too far in the distant future, there will be many, many more black tennis players playing . . . and they won't talk like me and they won't look like me and they won't act like me and they won't dress like me and they're going to upset a whole lot of people.

BUCHWALD:
I'm very optimistic about this country . . . Because when you see what countries are doing to people like me for just saying something, and . . . when you see what I'm getting in this country for doing the same thing, you tend to think that it's not a bad place. The thing about this country is if you attack the establishment and do it well, they make you a member of the establishment immediately.

MIKE WALLACE:
You've said the violin is a Jewish instrument. Why is it that so many fiddle players, so many world-class fiddle players, are Jewish? I mean, whether it's Oistrakh or Perlman or Heifetz or Menuhin or Isaac Stern?

PERLMAN:
You see, our fingers are circumcised, . . . which gives [them] very good dexterity, particularly in the pinky.

WILDER:
I don't set out to make a flop. I set out to make a hit. But, in the words of Mr. Goldwyn, "If people don't go to see a picture, nobody can stop them."

HOW I GOT FIRED AND FOUND *60 MINUTES*

In 1951 a truly spectacular piece of talent came over to TV from radio to produce not variety shows but news shows: Fred Friendly, a big bear of a man, arrived in lock step with Edward R. Murrow.

Friendly had produced Murrow's weekly radio show *Hear It Now,* which later became the *I Can Hear It Now* record albums, and he and Murrow, the two of them all but joined at the hip, were now about to launch a weekly TV show called *See It Now.* Before *60 Minutes*—seventeen years before *60 Minutes*—it was television's most prestigious broadcast. Along with it came awards and accolades and more applause than television had heard before. First thing you know, Friendly had replaced me at the head of the class.

That didn't bother me too much. Television was expanding, and I figured there was enough glory around for the two of us. Friendly, I think, didn't see it that way. I think he thought I was too big for my britches and that one of us had to go. When they made him president of CBS News—guess which one of us he decided had to go?

It was 1965 and *Douglas Edwards with the News* had become *The CBS Evening News with Walter Cronkite.* In Friendly's office was something I had never seen before and have never seen since—an escape hatch, a secret door through which he could depart surreptitiously if there was someone in his waiting room he didn't want to see. That day, however, there was someone he *did* want to see—me.

"Don," he said, "the Cronkite News is not big enough for you. You practically invented this business and I'm going to set up a special unit just for you."

I wasn't sure exactly what he was talking about but it sounded good. I went back to my glassed-in office, the one that looked out on the newsroom, and called my then wife, Frankie, and told her what Friendly had said about the Cronkite News not being big enough for me. "Don, dear," she said. Then I told her about the special unit he was going to create just for me.

"Don, dear," she said again.
"What?" I asked.
"You just got fired," she said.
Oh, my God, I thought. She's right!
The hot hand had cooled off. I was, despite the fancy talk about a special unit, relegated to the backwater to produce what, except for a few here and there, can best be described as hour-long snoozers.

Not everybody snoozed through documentaries. Most of the viewing public didn't even turn them on in the first place, although they said they did because they thought it gave them a certain cachet. When I was directing *See It Now* and bits and pieces of another prestige broadcast called *Omnibus*, people used to say to me, "Those are the only things we watch," but I knew it wasn't true. I knew they also watched *Gunsmoke* and *Wagon Train, I Love Lucy* and *Marcus Welby, M.D.* I know I did.

One of the snoozers Friendly put me in charge of was a series he himself had inaugurated called *Town Meeting of the World* on which we linked up world statesmen via satellite to talk to each other. To me, most of them sounded like Harold Macmillan or any one of those easily forgettable prime ministers the British squeezed in between Winston Churchill and Margaret Thatcher. Two of the few bright moments were provided by a Harvard professor named Kissinger, who showed considerable promise as a television performer, and an ex-sports announcer named Reagan, who also showed promise. Too bad they got sidetracked. They would have made a great anchor team. You couldn't say that for most of the others on that broadcast.

I have no objection to "talking heads" on television. In fact, I've always believed a good "talking head" with something to say is the best kind of television. But the "talking heads" on *Town Meeting* weren't, for the most part, very scintillating—and I sure as hell didn't want to do documentaries for the rest of my life. So, I began to think there had to be a way to make information more palatable.

I had by then figured out that what was principally wrong with documentaries was the name "documentary." No one likes to read documents so why would they want to watch something called a documentary? Years ago, long before television, a man named Pare Lorentz had made a film called *The River* and a man named Robert Flaherty had made a film called *Nanook of the North*. No one knew what to call them so they called them documentaries. The name stuck and when television came along, documentaries became the end-all and be-all of public affairs programming. The critics fairly salivated at the mention of the word "documentary"; good, bad or indifferent they loved them because to them they seemed to be a saintly kind of television—impersonal and often boring to everybody else but saintly to the critics.

Anyway, sometime in 1967 it dawned on me that if we split those public affairs hours into three parts to deal with the viewers' short attention span—not to mention my own—and came up with personal journalism (as Bill Moyers did later on for his documentaries) in which a reporter takes the viewer along with him on the story, I was willing to bet that we could take informational programming out of the ratings cellar. So I made a proposal to Richard S. Salant, who had become president of CBS News in 1966, after Friendly had a run-in with top management. "Why don't we try to package sixty minutes of reality as attractively as Hollywood packages sixty minutes of make-believe?" I asked him. (I didn't know then that *60 Minutes* was going to be the name of the program.)

The proposal was sent over to corporate headquarters, a black granite building that is known as "Black Rock." Word came back to make a pilot and if it worked out, maybe they would put it on every other Tuesday night at ten o'clock, alternating with documentaries and opposite top-rated *Marcus Welby, M.D.* That's what they did, and right off the bat we were a critical success, though our share of the audience was pitifully low. But *60 Minutes* was something the right people liked, and that was something the network brass liked.

Somewhere in the minds of the network brass, though, there must have been a faint hope that *60 Minutes* might be different from the usual snoozer; they moved us from Tuesday at ten to Sunday at six, which meant we didn't go on the air during the football season. But it was a better slot than the one opposite *Marcus Welby* and because six o'clock was an hour before prime time there was no way we could cause much trouble. Then in 1975, Oscar Katz, a vice president in the entertainment division, proposed that we move to seven o'clock. That's when we took off. That's when our percentage of the audience, which had been creeping up, began to impress the brass.

The trick has been not to lose the news buffs who make up our basic audience, while at the same time appealing to those I think of as the "Madames Defarges" who bring their knitting to the television set to watch heads fall into the basket just as they once brought their knitting to the guillotine. If you're a television producer, you kid yourself if you think you can make it without a fair share of them.

WALLACE REASONER

As *60 Minutes* began to take shape, first in my head, then on paper, then on film, I became more and more convinced that a new type of personal journalism was called for. *CBS Reports, NBC White Papers* and *ABC Closeups* seemed to me to be the voice of the corporation, and I didn't believe people were any more interested in hearing from a corporation than they were in watching a document. Harry Reasoner, I figured, was just the right guy to give it the personal touch, but I wasn't smart enough to realize that Reasoner teamed with Mike Wallace was precisely what I was looking for. My friend Bob Chandler was.

Chandler, a vice president of CBS News, asked if I had ever thought of using two guys.

"Like who?" I said.

"Like Reasoner and Wallace," Bob said.

That's what sent me to see Mike, whom I didn't know very well. He remembers our meeting this way:

> It was a Sunday afternoon and you and I went up to my fourth floor study. Reasoner, you told me, had been your first choice, but you agreed that what was called for was a little contrast . . . hence me.
>
> "What's it going to be about?" I asked you.
>
> "It's a magazine," you said. "You know, short pieces, long pieces, front of the book, back of the book, which will give you a chance to do interviews like the ones you used to do on *NightBeat*."

NightBeat was the television show Mike did before he came to CBS, the one that landed him on the cover of *Newsweek* and gave him a reputation as a tough interviewer. But toughness isn't what makes Mike Wallace Mike Wallace. Someone once said, "He brings out the best in everyone he works with." I knew that. Why do you think I was pitching him so hard? Mike says I was spewing out reasons why it should be a Reasoner-Wallace show so fast that he had trouble keeping up.

When I came up for air, Mike said he'd do it. Later, when I asked him why he had said yes, he said, "You were down on your luck after Friendly took you off the Cronkite News, but you were still the most imaginative guy around and you didn't take yourself too seriously. Besides, I was pretty sure I was going to Washington after the election to cover the Nixon White House so I could always get out of it." He didn't and that was seventeen years ago.

Harry remembers it this way: "In 1968, when Hewitt told me about this idea he had for a television magazine, I figured what the hell. I wasn't doing anything very exciting at the time and I figured I owed him one for our early days together on the Doug Edwards News. Even if it never got on the air—and it probably wouldn't—I didn't have anything to lose. It wasn't going to have much effect on my career, one way or the other, to do a pilot, so I said yes."

RICHARD M. NIXON
October 8, 1968

MIKE WALLACE:
There's been so much talk in recent years of style and charisma. No one suggests that either you or your opponent, Hubert Humphrey, has a good deal of it. Have you given no thought to this aspect of campaigning and of leading?

NIXON:
Well, when style and charisma connote the idea of contriving, of public relations, I don't buy it at all. As I look back on the history of this country, some of our great leaders would not have been perhaps great television personalities, but they were great Presidents for what they stood for . . . The most important thing about a public man is not whether he's loved or disliked but whether he's respected. And I hope to restore respect to the presidency at all levels by my conduct.

"NIXON"

Except for the Secret Service agents hanging around the lobby eyeing the people going in and out, it could have been any Fifth Avenue luxury co-op. In this case, however, the doorman who presided over the lobby, deciding who went up and who stayed down, had no choice but to hand over his power to the Feds. You got the feeling that, all things being equal, the tenants would have preferred it if Richard Nixon had bundled up his Secret Service agents and moved somewhere else. After all, some Rockefellers lived in the building and they never gave the doormen any trouble.

It didn't seem like much trouble to us. After a small wait, we got the nod. It was okay. Mr. Wallace and Mr. Hewitt were expected. The camera crew would please use the back elevator.

Mr. Nixon's valet, Manolo, greeted us and took us into a small sitting room to await the arrival of the candidate. Through the window and several stories below, we could see the Central Park Zoo. Mr. Nixon later told us he could hear the lions roar at night.

It was early October 1968, and the Republican nominee for President was gearing up for the final four weeks of the campaign. It had been eight years since Vice President Nixon lost to Senator Kennedy. This time he was the challenger and Hubert Humphrey, his opponent, was the incumbent Vice President. Mike had covered Nixon during the primaries leading up to his nomination and he liked Mike—liked him so much that after he won the election he offered him the job of White House Press Secretary. Mike was intrigued and flattered, as anyone would be, but I told him, "That doesn't make any sense. You don't want to go from being Mike Wallace to being a press secretary, even a White House press secretary. It's the kind of job a nobody takes so he can become a somebody." I don't know if that's what convinced Mike to stick with *60 Minutes*, but shortly after that conversation he told the Nixon people, thanks, but no thanks.

So, Nixon liked Mike all right, but he wasn't all that crazy about me. I had produced and directed the first Kennedy-Nixon debate in 1960 and although the make-up debacle that had dogged him through the campaign was the fault of his advisers, they blamed me. However, I did get indications in the intervening years that a "kiss and make up" session (no double entendre intended) was in order. The last time we had chatted was in 1964, before his speech introducing Barry Goldwater at the Republican Convention in San Francisco. He was being made up by CBS make-up artist Frances Arvold, whose services he had refused at the debate. As we sat in a small anteroom off the convention floor, I said, "You know, Mr. Nixon, if you had let Franny make you up four years ago there's a good chance Barry Goldwater would be going out there now to introduce you." I don't know whether he agreed or not, but he said he did.

Now it was 1968 and the man Nixon was facing had been the running mate of Lyndon Johnson, the man who had trounced Goldwater in 1964. Mike and I were discussing last minute details with our cameraman, Walter Dombrow, when Mr. Nixon arrived. After some of the usual pre-interview chitchat ("How you been?" "You look great!" "Remember what a nice time we had primary night in Oregon?"), Mike Wallace and Richard Nixon were ready to face each other. Mike, sensing that Nixon was ready for some candid talk, opened up by referring to 1960 and the fact that Nixon had not been the most loved man who ever ran for President. He stopped short of referring to him as "Tricky Dick," but you got the feeling Nixon wouldn't have minded, that he was prepared for anything, even that.

NIXON: As far as the charisma and all the PR tricks and everything else that's supposed to make you look like a matinee idol, forget it. If that's what they want in a President, I'm not the man.

WALLACE: But the name Nixon is an anathema to millions of American voters. To them Richard Nixon is a political opportunist to whom the desired political end has justified just about any political means. How does Richard Nixon, if elected by a majority, go about reconciling the doubts of the skeptics?

NIXON: I do have, based on a hard political career going back over twenty-two years, some people in this country who consider me an anathema, as you point out. But, on the other hand, I believe I have the kind of leadership qualities that can unite this country and that at least can win the respect if not the affection of those who have a very bad picture of Richard Nixon.

Richard Nixon's encounter with Mike Wallace didn't do either of them any harm. They both ended up with pretty good jobs. The next *60 Minutes* encounter with the Nixons was more social than cerebral. They agreed to let Mike and Harry Reasoner and our cameras take a look "upstairs" at the White House. It was a first. The American people had never before been upstairs at the White House. The tour was conducted by Tricia Nixon, who had some of that same little girl breathlessness that Jackie Kennedy had when she took television viewers on a tour of the downstairs.

Doing anything around the White House is a big deal. Where will you park the trucks? How will you get the camera cables up to the second floor? How much time do you need to set up? And we weren't doing anything as simple as disturbing the President in his office. We had to get the President out of his bed.

"I know what I can do with the President and Mrs. Nixon," Mrs. Nixon's press secretary said. "They can go to Camp David. But what'll I do with Julie?"

"Why don't you send her to the Mitchells and let Aunt Martha look after her," I said.

"That's not funny," she said. I thought it was, but the current troubles of Attorney General John Mitchell were taken very seriously. The Nixon White House was hardly a barrel of laughs. So I put on my serious face and managed to get the furniture moved, the rugs rolled up, and the President out of his house so we could tape our story.

The Monday after it was on the air I was having lunch in a restaurant near CBS called the Biarritz when the owner told me there was a phone call for me at the bar. I picked up the phone and a voice said, "Mr. Hewitt, the President is calling."

"I loved it," the President said.

"Thank you, Mr. President. We're very pleased that you liked it."

"Mrs. Nixon loved it."

"Very kind of you to say so, Mr. President." I wasn't taking any chances that it might not be the man, himself.

"Julie loved it."

"Julie loved it too? How nice, Mr. President."

After about the third "Mr. President" I noticed the bartender backing away, figuring he had a nutcake at his bar who thought he was talking to the President.

"Even Mamie called to say how much she liked it."

"Mamie liked it? That's swell, Mr. President." It went on more or less like that for a minute or so. All the time the bartender was getting more fidgety, and so was I. When "the President" finally hung up, I went back to the table and said to the guys I was having lunch with, "All right, who was that?"

"Who was what?" they said.

"The guy on the phone who sounded just like Nixon."

"How in hell do we know?" they said.

"Okay, wise guys," I said. "I know how to find out." It was going to be embarrassing, but I wasn't going to let them get away with it. I went back to the phone and called the White House. Now the bartender knew he really had a nut.

"White House," the voice on the phone said.

"Excuse me," I said, "but my name is Don Hewitt. Did you just place a call to me?"

"Just a minute, please," the White House operator said. Then a second operator came on the line.

"Mr. Hewitt?"

"Yes."

"I know the President was trying to reach you, but I thought we had completed that call."

"You did," I said. "I just wanted to make sure it was you."

Another President, Another Dinner

A couple of administrations later, I went to the White House with Morley Safer to cover a state dinner. During our prowling around the White House kitchen and the White House flower shop and the White House pantries and whatever else played a part in a state dinner we spent a lot of time with Gretchen Poston, Rosalynn Carter's social secretary, who was addicted to chocolate lollipops that she got from a candy store in Boston called See's.

That night after dinner, I was standing outside the East Gate in a dinner jacket sucking on a See's chocolate lollipop when Morley walked out accompanied by a very distinguished white haired gentleman. Morley introduced me to his companion, and told him: "Don is the Producer of *60 Minutes*."

"Well," the gentleman said, "it's a great pleasure to meet you."

"My pleasure," I said, "but I'm afraid I didn't catch your name."

"I'm Chief Justice Warren Burger," he said.

I almost choked on my lollipop. Morley says it was his most embarrassing moment.

IF THEY'D ONLY LISTENED TO ME

Back in the fifties we had a kid working in our film library who came to me and said he was leaving to manage a singer he had found in an obscure Brooklyn nightclub.

"Come on, Marty," I told him, "what do you know about managing a singer, and if she's an unknown, what do you need her for?" I suspected he had a crush on her, so I asked him to tell me about her.

"She's a skinny Jewish broad with a big nose," he said.

"That's just what you need in your life," I said, "a skinny Jewish broad with a big nose. Get rid of her!"

Next thing I knew Marty Ehrlichman had quit his job in the library and was managing the skinny Jewish broad with the big nose who went by the name of Barbra Streisand.

Wait, there's more:

Almost thirty years ago, when I was the producer-director of *Douglas Edwards with the News*, a producer at NBC, intrigued with the idea of being an on-air reporter, came to see me. I still remember her coming into my office and saying, "I want to be a broadcaster."

"Barbara," I said, "we're good friends, so I'll give it to you straight. With your voice, no one is going to let you broadcast." Barbara was Barbara Walters.

And how about this? When he was running our CBS Bureau in Washington, Howard K. Smith asked me to look at a broadcaster he thought had promise. I looked. "Forget him," I said. His name was Roger Mudd.

AGNEW:
By the time a year has gone by and I have been functioning in this expanded Vice President's role that has been given me . . . what I do and what I stand for are going to be so obvious that it's going to be very difficult for the people who are attempting to cast me in the role of the Neanderthal man to continue to think that way.

HARRY REASONER:
It is thirty-two years now since the Duke, then Edward VIII of Great Britain, left his throne to marry Wallis Simpson, the American divorcée . . . How old were you when you became king?

WINDSOR:
Forty-two.

REASONER:
And you were king for . . .

WINDSOR:
Ten months.

REASONER:
Is that long enough to be a king?

WINDSOR:
No.

MIKE WALLACE:
He is eighty years old, lives and works in Dallas, and is estimated to be worth anywhere from $400 million to $2 billion. Or, as one of his associates says, "Perhaps it's ten billion. Who knows?"
Hunt's fortune is mainly oil . . . He is probably the greatest rags-to-riches story of the twentieth century.
Give us a horseback guess as to how much H. L. Hunt is worth?

HUNT:
Well, you see, they talk about that I have an income of a million dollars a week . . . And that is a lot of percent erroneous.

WALLACE:
It is erroneous? It's bigger or smaller than that?

HUNT:
I would starve to death with an income of a million dollars a week.

H.L.

Mike had wanted to do H. L. Hunt real bad, but he was afraid old H.L. would be scared off by a phone call from him so Joe Wershba, who was going to produce the piece for Mike, wrote Hunt a letter telling him that *60 Minutes* had done Presidents and cardinals, and now wanted to do him. A few days later Mike called him. The voice on the other end was, as Mike remembers it, sad and a little wistful . . . not at all a billionaire's voice, whatever a billionaire's voice is. H.L. told Mike he was afraid Mike would take advantage of an old man. Now he sounded less like a billionaire than before. Mike, nonplussed for one of the few times in his life, put Wershba on the phone. Joe said, "Mr. Hunt, fear not. I haven't lost a billionaire yet." That did it. Joe had just made another friend. Someday I'd like to produce a show called "Friends of Joe Wershba." Most of them are gone now, but when they were around they included, along with H.L., Cardinal Cushing, Carl Sandburg, Jimmy Carter's sister Ruth Stapleton, Larry Flynt, Bill Loeb—the ultra right-wing New Hampshire publisher—and Alger Hiss. Joe always remained friends with the people he did stories about.

Joe's new friend H. L. Hunt said he would be happy to see Joe and Mike. So Joe flew to Dallas with cameraman Walter Dombrow to get the lay of the land. Joe remembers H.L. as a slightly stooped six-footer, a self-made billionaire who tended to be self-deprecating but was big on advice.

"The three greatest enemies of mankind," he told Joe, "are white flour, white bread and white sugar," although he made it clear that red people—not Indians but Communists—were worse. "Communists," he said, "want an end to the oil depletion allowance."

WALLACE: I gather that you're—I don't know if you were a high-school dropout or never even went to high school?

MR. HUNT: Well, I didn't go to high school, and I didn't go to grade school either. Education, I think, is for refinement and is probably a liability as far as making money.

WALLACE: One writer said about you: "When it comes to philanthropic works, H. L. Hunt is only about six cents more open-handed than Scrooge." What's your reaction to that?

MR. HUNT: Well now, he uses a very fancy expression, which I don't know what it means. I think the greatest philanthropy a person situated like I am can do is to furnish gainful employment to as many people as possible. I think that is the most useful thing that anyone can do with his money.

Health foods were a big thing with H.L., and he made sure his clerks pushed carrot cake in his food outlets. Once when Wershba was covering a *60 Minutes* story in Boston on black nationalism he was taken to a Muslim restaurant where they were pushing carrot cake. Joe couldn't wait to get to a phone and call H.L. "H.L.," he said, "the Muslims are big on carrot cake. They're your kind of people. Why don't you back them in a food chain?"

H.L. said he had once considered making loans to black farmhands, "but I figured communism would destroy the world before I could make farmers out of them, so I decided to put my money into fighting Communists instead." How much was H.L. really committed to saving America from communism? Barry Goldwater once said of him: "That old son-of-a-bitch never did give me more than three thousand dollars for my campaign."

No matter how hot the weather, and in Dallas it can get pretty hot, Mr. Hunt always wore a heavy dark-blue suit. He never said why and we never asked him. Maybe he thought wearing seersucker or gabardine was communistic. The suit had seen better days and so had his Oldsmobile. He always drove himself, and when he drove he talked with his hands, occasionally letting go of the wheel and going through most of the stop signs. "I've told the City Council a number of times there are at least a hundred and twenty-five signs in this city that just don't make sense and I do not intend to abide by them," he said. Then, revving up to seventy miles an hour, he added, "I suppose you gentlemen are kind of worried the way I'm driving."

"Oh, no," Walter Dombrow managed to gasp from the floor of the back seat.

"Well, I sure am," Hunt said. H.L. was not only rich, he was fun.

Every morning his wife, Ruth, who called him Popsi, packed a little brown bag with a sandwich on thick brown bread "made only from Smith County wheat" and dropped it on the seat of the Oldsmobile right beside him before he drove himself off to work. For dessert there was always carrot cake and "some sherbety ice cream." She also fed him fruit juices and meat loaf.

Once when the crew stopped at a general store on the way to one of Hunt's oil fields he started fingering the candy bars. "Would one of you gentlemen happen to have a quarter?" the richest man in Texas, if not in the world, asked sheepishly. Dombrow gave him a quarter and then when he asked for another quarter for another candy bar, Dombrow said, "Popsie is eating candy where Mumsie can't see him and if he doesn't stop, I'm going to tell."

Mumsie was Dombrow's name for Ruth, who kept whispering to Joe, "Remind Popsie about how we need a new car." So every chance he got, Joe would say, "H.L., it's time to get Ruth a new car." And H.L. would change the subject and say, "Joe, let me tell you about the Communist conspiracy to cut the oil depletion allowance."

The day after the *60 Minutes* story on Hunt was on the air, Ruth called Joe and said, "Joe, you know what's sitting out there in back of the house? Jes' a l'il old Lincoln Continental."

SAFER
WALLACE

It was November 11, 1970. Morley Safer was in Paris seeing to it that Charles de Gaulle was buried with proper ceremony. He was about to feed a satellite report to New York when the telephone rang in the control room and he was told it was Bill Leonard, then a vice president of CBS News. Says Morley:

> I couldn't imagine what Leonard could want. I assumed, as all reporters assume, that when the brass calls you, it is because you've screwed up. In fact I was sure of it. Probably some bit of minutia about De Gaulle. Everybody over a certain age was an expert on De Gaulle.
>
> When I completed my report, I gathered my thoughts, preparing to counterattack on anything he might say about De Gaulle, and I called him back.
>
> "How would you like to move to New York and take Reasoner's place, be the co-editor of *60 Minutes*? By the way, the De Gaulle stuff was very good."
>
> "Shit," I answered. "This is the phone call I would like to get five years from now."
>
> "We can't wait five years. Reasoner is leaving on Monday. Come to New York tomorrow."
>
> "I can't come tomorrow. Tomorrow we're burying De Gaulle."
>
> "Okay, the day after. 'Bye, have a nice funeral."
>
> I didn't. All I could think was:
>
> 1. I already had the best job in journalism. Chief of the London Bureau of CBS News—the exalted office once held by legends Edward R. Murrow, Charles Collingwood, Howard K. Smith, Eric Sevareid, Alexander Kendrick.
>
> 2. London was my oyster. I had an almost antique Rolls-Royce, the result of a remarkable streak of success at poker in Vietnam. I had turned forty just three days before the phone call, had been married for exactly two years, had a six-month-old daughter. My wife, Jane, had just completed gutting and renovating an Edwardian house in one of the prettiest squares in London and, in fact, was in the act of moving in while I was in Paris burying De Gaulle. There were, in short, good personal reasons for staying in London.
>
> 3. While it is every broadcast reporter's dream to work in a longer form than the one- or two-minute report demanded by the evening news broadcasts—why would I want to give up the dignity and importance of reporting for Walter Cronkite for the dubious honor of working for a fledgling television magazine that would surely have no staying power, that only went on the air every other Tuesday against the lovable Marcus Welby, M.D., and was run by the certifiably insane Don Hewitt. This proposition had all the appeal of winning an expenses paid vacation to Lagos.
>
> But I agreed on two conditions:
>
> 1. That my closest friend and perhaps the best cameraman ever to look through a viewfinder, John Tiffin, be made a *60 Minutes* producer (if I was going to fail, I was *not* going to fail alone) and
>
> 2. It would be written into my contract that when *60 Minutes* folded, I would be sent back to London. I'm still waiting.

THE POWER OF THE PRESS

It wasn't long after Morley joined *60 Minutes* that we found ourselves at the annual meeting of CBS television stations in Los Angeles, and one afternoon while driving around town, we stopped at an ice cream parlor called Clancy Muldoon's. Coming out with cone concoctions unknown to anyone except Angelenos, we got into our Hertz car and started to back out of the parking lot. Maneuvering with a marshmallow-fig-mint-peanut-something-or-other in one hand and a steering wheel in the other, I backed smack into a brand new Cadillac.

Uh-oh. Out steps a spectacular looking lady in tight jeans and spike heels. From the other side of the car out steps the biggest mother I ever saw. He's a very cool cat. She's roaring like a wounded lion. "Goddammit, can't you honkies see where you're going?"

"Ernestine, shut up and get back in the car. I'll handle it."

"Handle it, shit. Look at my fender. Fuckin' honkies must be blind."

"Ernestine, I said I'll handle it."

"Why the fuck they give blind honkies licenses anyway?"

"Ernestine, get back in the car."

With that, Mr. Six-foot-God-knows-how-many-inches starts at us.

"This is it," I said to Morley. "We're two dead honkies."

Then, almost as if God had reached down and parted the waters of the parking lot, Mr. Six-foot-etc. stopped dead in his tracks.

"Ain't you one of the dudes on *60 Minutes*?"

"Yes, sir, I'm Morley Safer."

"Ernestine, get out of the car and come over here and see who we done bumped into."

"Come over there, shit. Look at my goddamn fender."

"Ernestine, you hear me? You come over here and say hello to these two gentlemen."

His parting words? "We're terribly sorry if we caused you gentlemen any trouble."

The power of the press.

FELLINI:
If there is a little wisdom in becoming older and older, I think it is just to forget to try to know who you are. To try and know who you are in terms of moralism, in terms of idealism, you lose time. When you know that you are exactly so-and-so, so what?

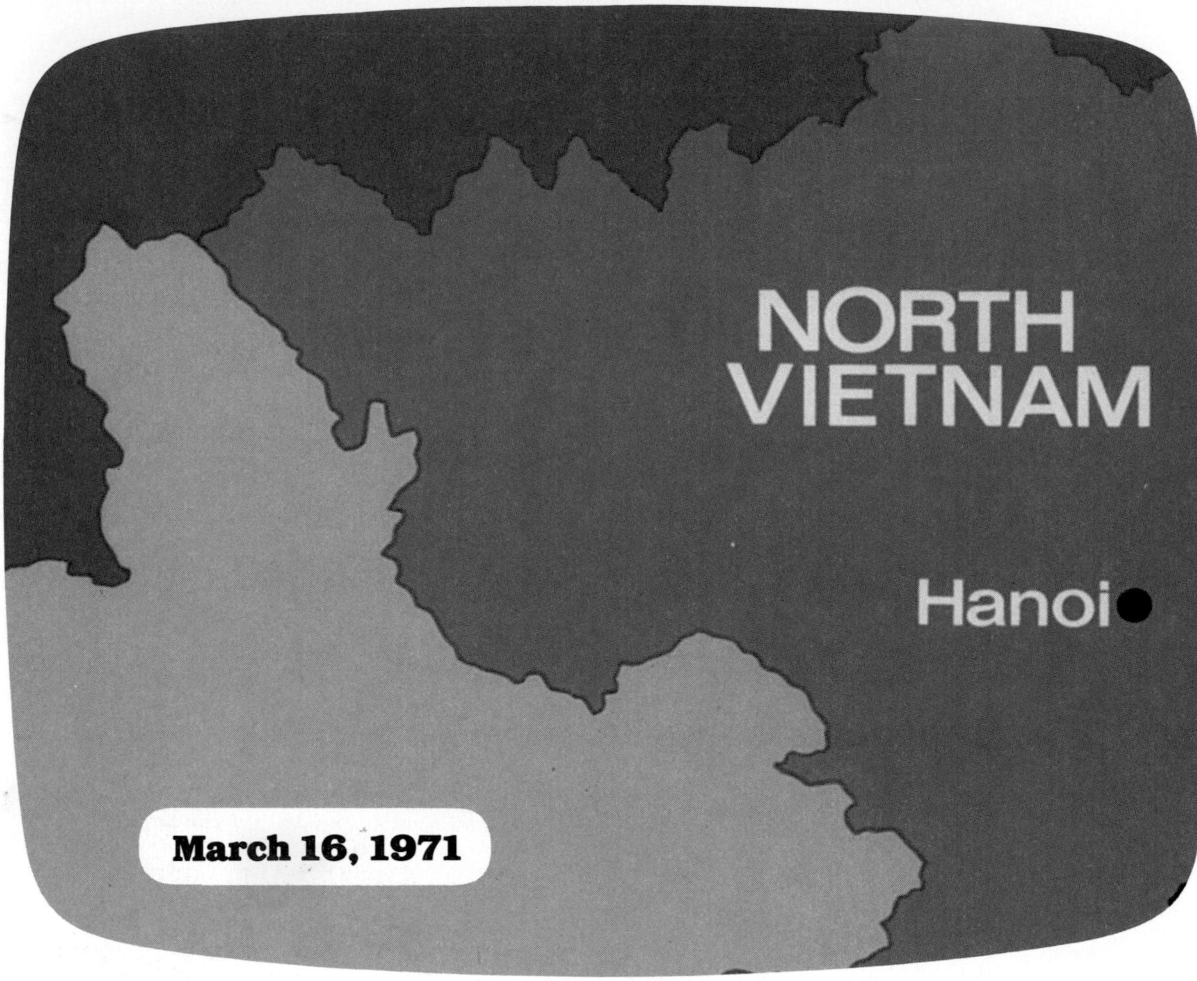

NORTH VIETNAM

Hanoi

March 16, 1971

"WHAT REALLY HAPPENED AT THE GULF OF TONKIN?"

MORLEY SAFER: The date: August 4, 1964. For most people it triggers no particular emotion. It is no December 7, 1941. But August 4 is important whether you remember the date or not. It was on that date in the Gulf of Tonkin, off the coast of North Vietnam, that the American war in Vietnam really began. And the incident that began it has become as controversial as the war itself. The U.S. destroyers *Maddox* and *Turner Joy* were attacked by Communist torpedo boats. Or were they? . . .

It is now six years and seven months since the Tonkin incident and the Tonkin Resolution. The incident produced the [congressional] resolution, and the resolution was quite simple. It gave the President the right to protect American troops in Vietnam with whatever means he felt necessary, the power to prevent further aggression by North Vietnam and to prevent South Vietnam from falling to the Communists. Few people at the time thought it would take more than six years and almost 45,000 dead Americans—and more—to achieve those ends. Boys who were twelve years old that August died last week in Vietnam.

Let's go back to August 4 and the U.S. Destroyer *Maddox* and try to find out what happened that night in the Gulf of Tonkin.

In July of 1964, units of the 7th Fleet were patrolling the South China Sea off the coast of Vietnam. The United States was not at war with North Vietnam, but it was helping South Vietnam with massive economic and military aid. Then . . . Sunday afternoon, August 2nd. It happened. The *Maddox* against three North Vietnamese PT boats. The North Vietnamese said the *Maddox* invaded their waters and they chased her out. The United States says that the *Maddox* was in neutral waters, that although the *Maddox* fired first, it was in self-defense when the North Vietnamese PT boats were about to attack. We're fairly sure all three PT boats were hit and none of the torpedoes hit the *Maddox*. But the *Maddox* very likely was hit. There was a bullet hole in the aft gun director. It was repaired later and painted over, no sign of it today.

But two nights later, the night of the controversial battle, the *Maddox* did not take any damage or suffer any losses, which is but one of many reasons why Senate investigators now believe there never was any battle that night.

The *Maddox* and the *Turner Joy* reported that they were ambushed at the beginning of the evening by perhaps five or six torpedo boats . . . The President was assured an attack had taken place, even though Captain [John] Herrick on board the *Maddox* still had his doubts. [Herrick was the officer in charge of the destroyer division which included the *Maddox* and the *Turner Joy*.] Herrick cabled: ENTIRE ACTION LEAVES MANY DOUBTS EXCEPT FOR APPARENT ATTEMPTED AMBUSH AT BEGINNING. SUGGEST THOROUGH RECONNAISSANCE IN DAYLIGHT BY AIRCRAFT.

And at 1:30 A.M. [a message was sent that] could have changed history. It showed Captain Herrick even more doubtful: REVIEW OF ACTION MAKES MANY RECORDED CONTACTS AND TORPEDOES FIRED APPEAR DOUBTFUL. FREAK WEATHER EFFECTS, AND OVEREAGER SONAR MEN MAY HAVE ACCOUNTED FOR MANY REPORTS. NO ACTUAL VISUAL SIGHTINGS BY MADDOX. SUGGEST COMPLETE EVALUATION BEFORE ANY FURTHER ACTIONS.

But the White House and the Pentagon and Pacific Headquarters kept pressing Captain Herrick for absolute certainty immediately. At 2:45 A.M. Tonkin time, Herrick to headquarters: DETAILS OF ACTION PRESENT A CONFUSING PICTURE, ALTHOUGH CERTAIN ORIGINAL AMBUSH WAS BONA FIDE. . .

We asked [Captain Herrick] to return to the *Maddox*, now a training ship, and recall the confusing events of August 4, 1964 . . . Your original messages to the Pentagon in Washington did leave some doubt, is that correct?

HERRICK: They were intended to. I wanted to have a little time to interview the CO of the *Maddox* and the *Turner Joy* and to accumulate the information necessary to arrive at a logical conclusion of what happened that night. And after that information was in, then I verified my previous reports and stated that I definitely felt that we had been attacked that night.

SAFER: It's also been suggested that Washington was putting a great deal of pressure on you to come up with some positive answers to what happened that night. A positive answer being, "Yes, we were attacked."

HERRICK: Well, I'm sure they needed one. And that's what we were trying to obtain for them and we did and sent it in.

SAFER: By six o'clock that evening in Washington, President Johnson had given the final go-ahead for the bombing of North Vietnam . . . And yet, while 7th Fleet pilots were preparing to attack, the Pentagon was still pressing the Commander in Chief of the Pacific, Admiral Sharp, to press Captain Herrick on the *Maddox* to, in McNamara's words, "make damn sure there had been an attack."

Admiral Sharp to Herrick: (1) CAN YOU CONFIRM ABSOLUTELY THAT YOU WERE ATTACKED? (2) CAN YOU CONFIRM SINKING OF PT BOATS? (3) DESIRE REPLY DIRECTLY WITH SUPPORTING EVIDENCE.

Captain Herrick's final report [came] shortly after 8:00 P.M., Washington time; he still had doubts: MADDOX SCORED NO KNOWN HITS AND NEVER POSITIVELY IDENTIFIED A BOAT. NO KNOWN DAMAGE OR PERSONNEL CASUALTIES TO EITHER SHIP. TURNER JOY CLAIMS SINKING ONE BOAT AND DAMAGING ANOTHER. THE FIRST BOAT TO CLOSE MADDOX PROBABLY FIRED TORPEDO AT MADDOX, WHICH WAS HEARD BUT NOT SEEN. ALL SUBSEQUENT MADDOX TORPEDO REPORTS WERE DOUBTFUL IN THAT IT IS SUPPOSED THAT SONAR MAN WAS HEARING SHIP'S OWN PROPELLER BEAT.

But by now it's all academic. President Johnson goes on television shortly before midnight to announce the bombing of North Vietnam. The next day at the United Nations, Ambassador Adlai Stevenson explains American action and calls for world support. Two days later, Congress passes the Tonkin Resolution. It gives the President authority to take America deep into Vietnam and open war, without a declaration of war. The President would later refer to the Tonkin Gulf Resolution as his authority for the actions he took in Vietnam.

Because the Gulf of Tonkin story was one in which we pointed a finger at a President of the United States and suggested that he had played fast and loose with the people, it should have made a big splash. It didn't, because back in 1971 *60 Minutes* was in a very small pond. If we had run it ten years later, when ten times as many people would have seen it, just as sure as 7:00 P.M. Sunday comes around once a week somebody would have jumped up and down demanding equal time and hollering that we were communists or, at the very least, communist sympathizers, whatever they are.

JOHNSON:
Throughout our history, our public has been prone to attach Presidents' names to international difficulties. You will recall the War of 1812 was branded Mr. Madison's war; and the Mexican War was Mr. Polk's war; and the Civil War or the War Between the States was Mr. Lincoln's war; and World War I was Mr. Wilson's war; and World War II was Mr. Roosevelt's war; and Korea was Mr. Truman's war; and President Kennedy was spared that . . . because in his period [Vietnam] was known as Mr. McNamara's war. And then it became Mr. Johnson's war, and now they refer to it as Mr. Nixon's war . . . I think it's very cruel to have that burden placed upon a President.

LYNDON

LBJ stories are legion at CBS. There was the time he decided to go on the air in a hurry and there was no one to make him up but a kid who worked in our Washington bureau. It was a lousy make-up job, and after he got off the air the President sent a Secret Service agent out to the CBS remote truck parked in the driveway near the Oval Office.

"You," the agent said to young Mike Honeycutt. "The President wants to see you."

As Honeycutt tells it, he arrived in the Oval Office and stood nervously shifting from one foot to the other in front of the presidential desk until the President of the United States looked up from something he was signing and said, "Boy, you trying to fuck me?"

"Sir?" was about all Honeycutt could blurt out. Then the President said to one of his agents, "Get him out of here." Honeycutt says he was sure the President was going to add, "Shoot him."

The first time I saw LBJ outside of the Oval Office, Martin Agronsky and I had gone to the White House to keep a date at nine o'clock in the evening with George Christian, LBJ's press secretary, to talk about doing a live broadcast of LBJ answering questions about Vietnam to be posed by the governors, who were coming to Washington to have dinner at the White House. To kill time Agronsky had driven a friend to the airport and I had stopped at the Madison Hotel for dinner. After dinner I wandered slowly over to the White House so as not to get there before our nine o'clock appointment.

As I meandered up the driveway toward the press office entrance a nervous aide was waiting in the doorway. "Where's Agronsky?" he asked.

"He went to the airport," I said.

"What do you mean, 'he went to the airport'?"

"What do you mean 'what do I mean'? He went to the airport. What's so difficult to understand about that?"

"The President," the aide said, "is waiting upstairs for the two of you for dinner."

Jesus, I thought.

Sure enough, the President was waiting for us for dinner, and he was hungry, even if I wasn't. Agronsky, who had also had dinner, arrived a short time later.

We talked about what he wanted us to do on the broadcast, and then he picked up the phone alongside him at the table and told the White House operator to get him Bess Abell, the White House social secretary.

"Bess," he told her, "you're going to have to cancel the performance of *Hello, Dolly!* that we scheduled for the governors' dinner." The next thing I knew, he was saying, "Calm down, Bess. Hewitt says he can't do what he wants to do with all those sets and actors in the East Room." With that, he handed me the phone.

The White House social secretary was furious.

"What do you think you're doing?" She asked.

"I'm not doing anything, Bess. The President is. This is his idea, not mine."

After a few minutes of Bess's tongue lashing, I told the President that she wanted to speak to him again. He told me he had nothing to tell her and that I should handle it. I didn't know how to handle it, so I hung up.

The only other eventful thing that happened brought me out of my chair. All of a sudden a buzzer went off. My God, the hot line; it's World War III, I thought. You know what it was? The President's battery-operated pepper mill. You've never seen a battery-operated pepper mill? Neither had I. And I've never seen once since.

That was just before the President noticed it was time for the eleven o'clock news. A White House butler rolled in a TV set and turned it to one of the local channels just as the newscaster proclaimed, "The President said today that he would make an important speech tomorrow."

"I did not," the President said, addressing the TV set. "Never said it was important." And then for the next few minutes he carried on a conversation with the television set as if the newscaster were there with us at the table. It was some performance. Every time the guy paused, the President interjected a comment. It would have made a great bit on *Saturday Night Live.*

After midnight, as Agronsky and I were strolling down the driveway toward the guardhouse to leave the White House grounds, I told him, "This broadcast is never going to happen."

"Are you nuts?" Agronsky said. "Would he have spent all this time with us if it weren't going to happen?"

"It's not going to happen," I said.

"How you figure that?" Martin asked.

"When Mrs. Johnson hears that he wants to turn *Hello, Dolly!* into *Hello, Lyndon!* she'll nix it. Asking the governors to sing for their supper is a lousy idea."

Agronsky looked at me like I had lost my mind, but the next day I got a call from George Christian, LBJ's press secretary.

"It's off," he said.

"Why?" I asked.

"Mrs. Johnson thought it was a lousy idea."

You haven't been put in your place until you've been put in your place by Lyndon Johnson, as I was the morning before we taped the *60 Minutes* story on the LBJ library in Austin, Texas.

I had been at the LBJ Ranch one other time, with Cronkite, to do a broadcast on Lady Bird. What I mostly remember about that first visit was the President wandering around in his long johns hollering: "Bird, where are my shirts?"

What I wasn't prepared for on the second trip was to have the former President and Mrs. Johnson come to the airport to meet us and drive us to the ranch, where we were to spend the night. Not a bad limo service. Mike and I got into the jump seats.

Bud Benjamin, who was producing one of those LBJ-Cronkite conversations and was traveling with us, sat on the back seat with President and Mrs. Johnson. It didn't matter that LBJ was no longer in office, he was still "Mr. President."

After dinner we were shown to a bunkhouse to bed down (I think that's what you do on a ranch—"bed down for the night"). The next morning, after breakfast, the President took us for a tour of his ranch in his famous white Lincoln convertible, with the top down.

Bud rode up front with the President, Mike and I sat in the back and that's when he decided to put me in my place, to show this Fancy Dan TV producer that he was the boss. (Come on, Lyndon! Anybody who's ever been within ten feet of you knows that.) He stopped the car, turned to me in the back seat, and handed me the wrapper of the candy bar he was munching.

Like young Mike Honeycutt, all I could think to say was, "Sir?"

"You," he said. "Throw the wrapper in that can!"

Mike and Bud were grinning. I didn't know what to do so I grinned too, got out and did what the President told me to do. I put the candy wrapper in the garbage can. When I turned around he had driven away leaving me to run after the car. After about a quarter of a mile, he stopped so I could get back in.

After that the President drove us to a tumbledown shack in the Lyndon Johnson State Park, got out and pushed a button that activated a loudspeaker in a tree, and the four of us sat in the car and listened to the tree tell us a story. As best I can recall, it went like this: "A little old black midwife left this cabin one stormy night and rode a mule through the thunder and lightning a mile or two down the road to deliver a little baby." As the tree got to the punch line, LBJ turned around to me and Mike in the back seat. I couldn't look him in the eye so I concentrated on the big ears sticking out from under his Stetson, as the tree said: "And that little baby's name was Lyndon Baines Johnson."

There he was, looking right in our faces, and I didn't know what in hell to say. Maybe he wanted us to applaud. Leave it to Mike. Straight-faced, and with his best delivery, he said, "Mr. President, that's the loveliest story I ever heard."

After our morning at the ranch, Mike and I preceded the President down to the offices of the local television station he and Mrs. Johnson owned. We were to pick him up before going over to the library.

As we were being shown around, a voice came over the PA system: "Now hear this! President Johnson has arrived, and the eggs are in the waiting room."

"What the hell is that all about?" I asked our escort.

"Oh," he said, "the President always brings us eggs from the ranch."

"How nice," I said.

"How nice, hell," he said. "He sells them to us."

When we arrived at the library, the cameramen were still lining up their shots, and Mike, LBJ and I sat on a low wall two stories above the marble entry floor.

"I think we ought to talk about Vietnam," Mike told the President.

"No, Mike," he said. "I talked about Vietnam enough when I was President. I don't want to talk about that anymore."

"You're wrong, Mr. President," Mike said. "I think we should talk about Vietnam."

"Goddammit, Mike," he said, "I'm not going to talk about Vietnam, so stop mentioning it."

"Mr. President," Mike said, "I still think you should talk about Vietnam."

"Oh, oh," I thought, "he's going to knock both of us over this wall down onto that marble floor two stories below."

He didn't. But I don't know why he didn't. He was mad enough to do it.

The other thing that I guess would have made him mad was to probe him about what he knew about the Kennedy assassination. Maybe he didn't know anything more than what had been made public, but coming back from Texas on the plane I thought maybe we should have at least raised the question, whether he got mad or not.

It's not that I subscribe to any of the conspiracy theories that kicked around for years after that terrible day, but once, sitting on the terrace at Hickory Hill with Bobby Kennedy—just the two of us—I asked if he believed Lee Harvey Oswald all by himself had killed his brother.

Bobby's answer surprised me. "What difference does it make?" he said. "It won't bring him back."

I never believed that Bobby believed it made no difference. His answer is the reason I never subscribed to any of the conspiracy theories. If there had been a conspiracy, the President's brother, who had been Attorney General, would have had the most reason and the most clout to discover it. If *he* didn't, I believe there was nothing to discover, and that "What difference does it make?" was his way of telling me there wasn't.

So, I don't think LBJ could have revealed any conspiracy. But he just might have known what Earl Warren, who ran the investigation, meant when he said, "We may not know the whole story in our lifetime." I'm still curious about that.

AGNELLI:
There are many ways of dying. I don't think an accident is the worst. My father died in an airplane crash. My mother died in a motor-car crash. I think, of the many ways one can see people finished, there are some infinitely duller and more unpleasant ways.

MIKE WALLACE:
Were there any witnesses to your meetings with Howard Hughes?

IRVING:
Yes, there were . . . My researcher . . . who accidentally happened to be sitting with me in a room when Hughes arrived too early. He stood there. Hughes stood there. I stood there. And finally I said, "Well, this is my assistant, who's doing some research for me on a project." And Hughes said, "I suppose you know who I am." My researcher . . . started to stick out his hand, then withdrew it instantly because Hughes is not very keen on shaking hands. And then, after another moment of awkward silence, Hughes reached into his pocket and pulled out a bag . . . and said . . . "Have a prune." And my researcher took a prune and said, "This is an organic prune, isn't it?" Hughes said, "Yes, yes. How did you know? This is the only kind I eat. All the rest are poison."

"WILL THE REAL HOWARD HUGHES . . ."

One day in 1972, Bill Brown, a *60 Minutes* producer, told me he had heard there was a guy in town who had interviewed Howard Hughes. "He's seen him," Bill said, "and he says he's got long fingernails, a scraggly beard and walks around in Kleenex boxes instead of slippers."

"Either you're nuts or this guy is nuts," I told him.

"You want to meet him?" Bill said.

"No," I said, "because I don't believe he exists."

He existed all right. And when it was announced that *Life* magazine had signed him to do an article about his meetings with Howard Hughes, I had to eat crow.

"Want to meet him?" Bill asked once again.

"You bet," I said.

"Come on, then," Bill said. "My friend, Marty Ackerman, has him stashed away on the third floor of his mansion on Park Avenue." Ackerman had owned the *Saturday Evening Post* at one time and had acquired the house as part of the settlement when the magazine folded. Later, the East German U.N. delegation took it over.

The Ackermans invited Mike and Bill and me to have lunch with their house guest, Clifford Irving. Also at lunch was a lawyer for *Life* who was there to draw up a contract.

I was skeptical, and told Irving that I thought he was a phony. He smiled, but the *Life* magazine lawyer was furious. "What kind of a fool do you think *Life* magazine is?" he asked.

I said I thought Irving, having seen what could be done with art forgery while researching and writing his 1969 book called *Fake: The Story of Elmyr de Hory, the Greatest Art Forger of Our Time,* had decided to try a literary forgery.

The *Life* magazine lawyer got madder and madder and said, "You must think we're naïve."

"Don't get so upset," I told him. "I think the whole thing is funny." So did Bill, but Mike, who was usually skeptical of stories like this one, bought it hook, line and sinker, and two days later we taped the Mike Wallace–Clifford Irving interview.

With the big CBS remote truck parked outside Ackerman's house, I told the crew that if anyone stopped and asked what we were doing, to tell them we were making a commercial. At this point only we and *Life* knew the whereabouts of Clifford Irving, the man who had seen Howard Hughes.

As everyone knows, Clifford Irving turned out to be a fake, but that somehow made our interview even better. By the time we ran it, the fraud was common knowledge, and to punctuate some of his more outlandish tales, we ran them a second time as instant replays. Irving thought that was rubbing it in and was sore as hell. I told him that if anybody should be sore, it was us, and we weren't. "How do you have the nerve to be?" I asked him. He didn't have any answer to that.

On the next couple of pages is some more of the interview.

WALLACE: In his younger days, Hughes developed a reputation as a ladies' man. I asked Irving about that.

IRVING: Well, he's known them all, you know—Ava Gardner, Linda Darnell, Katharine Hepburn.

WALLACE: I wasn't sure from reading the book whether his relationship with Miss Hepburn was an affair of the heart or an affair of the head, if you will.

IRVING: I think it was an affair of the heart and the head. He's very respectful of Katharine Hepburn. He liked her very much. He said—he said, "She was a very clean woman, used to bathe three or four times a day, and she always told me that I was divine." He said, "And I kind of liked that."

WALLACE: I understand that he has a kind of classification system for the human beings with whom he comes in contact?

IRVING: Yes, he had a system. I'm not sure if he employs it anymore. It was a whole file card. And all his friends and associates, anyone who might fly on his planes and meet him, had a classification: A–B–C–D. And that ranged from filthy, moderately dirty, dirty and moderately clean.

WALLACE: One hears the stories that he's, you know, with long hair and long fingernails, and a pretty decrepit-looking person himself.

IRVING: This is nonsense.

WALLACE: What—when you last saw him—what did he look like?

IRVING: Hughes is a man almost as tall as I am, six foot three.

WALLACE: Weighs?

IRVING: Under a hundred and forty pounds.

WALLACE: Is he a good-looking man, still?

IRVING: He has the good looks of a man who once was extremely handsome and has dignity in his face.

WALLACE: Does he wear a beard?

IRVING: Not a real one.

WALLACE: Not a real one?

IRVING: What I mean is he has on occasion worn false beards and false mustaches and wigs.

WALLACE: With you?

IRVING: Mike, I said there's a James Bond setup here that's out of the worst possible detective novel you could ever read.

WALLACE: Well, now, he wears beards and wigs and disguises?

IRVING: Well, he doesn't wear them in my presence; he takes them off when he arrives. But he's worn them.

WALLACE: Just so people would not—

IRVING: When I met him the second time in Puerto Rico, he had suddenly grown a full head of hair. And I said, "What's that?" He said, "Oh, it's a wig. I bought it at the five-and-dime. It cost me nine ninety-five." He said, "I have to watch out." He says, "There are people always looking for me. And there's a price on my head." So he uses these disguises.

WALLACE: Do I understand that he has some kind of a double who has the same symptoms that he has?

IRVING: He did for a time have a man who, as he said, like the fool at the sultan's table, tried out the medicines that he had to take.

WALLACE: Why?

IRVING: Well, it's a bit extreme. And I suppose he was afraid, at that particular time, that there were certain people who would like to see him out of the way. At least, that's his story.

WALLACE: Irving says the last time he saw Howard Hughes was on December 7. Since that time, a voice purported to be that of Howard Hughes has told reporters that he doesn't know Irving and that the whole business of the so-called autobiography is a fraud.

Have you tried to be in touch with him since? Have you tried to tell him, "Mr. Hughes, come forward and say this"?

IRVING: I've said, "Howard, speak up. Get, you know, call off the dogs." I've written him a letter to the only address that I have at the moment that I know is valid. And I've used the correct code words for identification. And if he gets that letter, which apparently he hasn't so far, I presume he will surface.

I don't know why he hasn't surfaced. It puzzles me. It upsets me. It distresses me. And I don't mean on my own account, because I can handle this. And we have the proof, and that's no problem. It just distresses me that—that he seems unable to respond.

WALLACE: There's no doubt in your mind that he's alive, is there?

IRVING: No, I assume he's alive.

LOOKING FOR HOWARD HUGHES

The Clifford Irving affair sparked a lot of interest in finding Howard Hughes for real. So, one day Morley and I got on a plane and went to Las Vegas to see if we could pick up his trail. We called the story "One of Our Billionaires Is Missing" and we nosed around a little, shot some film in front of a few of the landmark hotels Hughes had owned. We were standing around with the crew outside a phone booth on the strip waiting for a call back from Robert Maheu, who had been Hughes's top man in Nevada, when a Vegas show girl in a bikini walked by in high heels.

"What's the big deal?" our soundman asked. He was older than the rest of us.

"You blind?" I said.

"No, not blind," he said, "but I think that stuff they gave us during World War Two to make us less horny is beginning to work."

Maheu called back and we went to see him. The first thing he said when we walked into his house was, "Hughes is having you followed."

"What makes you think so?"

"I don't think so," he said. "I know so, because my guys are tailing his guys and his guys are tailing you."

We spent the better part of an afternoon in Maheu's living room hearing his side of the story about why Hughes had fired him from his $600,000-a-year job. Maheu was an ex-FBI agent and had run the Hughes gambling empire for some years, but, he told us, he had never met the man and had only laid eyes on him once, when they brought him on a stretcher by train to Las Vegas.

When we got back to the Sands, where we were staying, Morley went to take a nap and I went into the casino to play twenty-one. I was there a half hour or so when Sam Zelman, the *60 Minutes* producer on the story, walked in and said, "Strange thing just happened. I found a message in my box to call a number in Los Angeles and figured I'd better call from a phone booth outside the hotel."

"And?" I said.

"And the man who answered the phone said, 'You, Hewitt, Safer. Century Plaza Hotel, Saturday morning, eleven A.M. No cameras. No mikes.' Should we go?"

"How can we not?" I asked.

The next morning we flew to Los Angeles, took a cab to the Century Plaza and went up to the room we were told to go to. Waiting for us were Bill Gay, executive vice president of Hughes Tool, and Hughes's lawyer, Chester Davis.

"Sit down," Gay said. "We thought we'd like to tell you our side of the Maheu story."

Then they proceeded to rebut everything Maheu had told us.

Wow! I thought. They've got Maheu's house bugged!

Then I thought, We've gotten to the top men in the Hughes organization. Maybe they'll take us to the man.

"No can do," they said.

The person who gave us the most dope on Hughes was Hank Greenspun, who owned the Las Vegas *Sun*. He told us, among other things, about Howard Hughes's insomnia and how, when he didn't like a late night movie he was watching on one of the Las Vegas television stations, he just up and bought the station. But I'd heard that before. In fact, Hank had little to tell us that he himself hadn't already published.

If I was going to learn anything new about the mystery man, I would have to go to the Bahamas, where Hughes was holed up on the top floor of the Britannia Beach Hotel. Or was he? To get to Hughes's floor, I had to have a ploy. It wasn't going to be easy. Hughes's guards had sealed off an entire corridor. I sent up a note that said: "If you're curious about Clifford Irving, I've spent a lot of time with him and can fill you in." That, I thought, might do it. I waited two days for an answer. When none came I just got in the elevator and went up. As I got off the elevator, the guards were otherwise occupied and the floor was full of moving men. I ducked into a closet and left the door open just enough to see what was going on. Being carried out was a cheap Naugahyde couch, a lot of kitchen utensils, some movie-editing equipment, a plasma holder and a hospital bed.

Could it be, I thought, that this is all baloney. That Hughes has never been here and that the moving out, like the moving in, is an act to draw fire away from where he really is? If he's so sick that he needs a hospital bed, I thought, why isn't he in it?

About that time, a guard caught me and escorted me to the elevator. I noticed that the stuff the moving men were carrying had gone onto the freight elevator so I went around to the back of the hotel, where they were offloading it and piling it into a van. If that's really his stuff, I thought, all I have to do is follow it to find out where he is.

I found a cab in front of the hotel.

"Ever see a movie called *The French Connection*?" I said to the driver.

"Yeah man, it was good."

"Remember the stake-out scene? Well, that's what you and I are going to do. There's a large truck parked behind the hotel, and when it leaves we're going to follow it."

"Yes, boss," he said.

I got in the back of the cab and went to sleep. It was after midnight when the driver woke me. "The truck is leaving," he said.

"Follow it."

Several miles out of town, the truck turned onto a lonely dirt road near the airport. It led to a hangar at the far end of the field. The cab driver stopped and said there was no way he was going to follow the truck down that dirt road in the middle of the night.

"Okay, wait here," I said. "I'll walk down the road myself." I got about a hundred yards down the road and decided this was a good way to get myself killed, so I went back to the cab and told the driver to take me to the control tower.

When I walked in, there was only one man on duty. "You can't come in here," he said.

I put a twenty-dollar bill in front of him and he changed his mind. "What can I do for you?" he asked.

"Nothing," I told him. "I just want to sit here and wait."

About 4 A.M. a cargo plane landed and taxied up to the hangar where the truck had unloaded Hughes's junk from the hotel. After the plane loaded up, the pilot called the tower and filed a flight plan for Fort Lauderdale. That's what I was after. I went downstairs and found an office where a guy was sleeping with his feet up on the desk. "Can I use the phone?"

"Be my guest," he said.

I called the CBS News radio desk in New York and had them record me. My story began: "Howard Hughes moved out of the Bahamas this morning and is now heading for Fort Lauderdale, or at least his worldly possessions are." Then I gave them some more and the number of the plane and its estimated arrival time, and told them that if they followed what came off the plane, it might lead them to Howard Hughes.

I thanked the guy with his feet up on the desk for the use of the phone. Then he thanked me. "I'm the Associated Press stringer down here," he said, "and I suspected something was going on, but I didn't know what until I listened to your phone call."

Oh well, easy come easy go. There went my exclusive.

The next day I decided to try and get a look at the top floor of the hotel that Hughes had just vacated. Around the back I noticed a bunch of painters ready to go up. So I went and got me some white pants, a white shirt, a bucket of paint and a brush, and got on the freight elevator they were using. There was something I wanted to know. I went into what someone told me had been Hughes's bedroom and listened. Down below you could hear the kids in the pool and the drunks around the bar. That's what I wanted to know. I figured, there and then, that Hughes would never stay in a room that was that noisy, and I concluded that my original hunch was right. He had never been there, and the guards and electronic equipment on the roof were all a smoke screen. Several years later it was reported that he died on a plane en route back to the States, but my guess has always been that he had died long before, and it was to somebody's advantage to keep the myth going that Hughes was still alive. Whose? That's the part I never figured out.

OUR MAN IN HAVANA

Bill Brown, the *60 Minutes* producer who led us to Clifford Irving, was handsome and fun to be with, and although he wasn't and never had been, people thought he was an agent the CIA had planted in our shop. To do what? I haven't the slightest idea. There were always stories like that, and to this day there are those who think our phones are tapped. I don't believe it. What are they going to find out? Anything we know we put on the air. But just the fact that people thought Bill was an agent gave him a mystique. He worked mostly with Mike and he had a wonderful way of finding great characters like Clifford Irving and Otto Skorzeny, the SS colonel Hitler had sent to rescue Mussolini. Having dinner with Skorzeny, Bill said, was like listening to Mel Brooks. Once in a restaurant in Madrid, Skorzeny said, "You know, Bill, Josef Goebbels was a very nice man but he set a very poor table." Another time he said, "I never knew what the Führer saw in Eva Braun. She was shtupid."

Who better than Bill Brown to go with us to Havana to make contact with Castro? That's what Mike and I did in 1970.

In Mexico City, where we had to change planes, everybody on the Havana flight was photographed as he went aboard.

"What's that for?" I asked.

"We want to make sure that the passenger who goes in is the same passenger who comes out," a Mexican immigration official told me.

"You mean," I said, "there's a chance they could keep Mike and me and send two other guys back masquerading as us?"

"You got it," he said.

Hanging around Havana's National Hotel, where they put us up, were a bunch of Americans known as the Venceramos Brigade, who were in Cuba to help Fidel cut sugar cane. In the group was a woman Mike knew who edited a radical magazine in Greenwich Village. It didn't matter that we were representatives of the capitalist press, we were faces from home; and Mike's friend, the radical activist, told us she wished she had known we were coming because we could have brought her a "Care Package." She'd been there for months and what she wanted most, she said, was her diaphragm and a box of Milky Ways.

The hotel had seen better days. Each room had a bathroom with a sink, a tub and a toilet, but no toilet seat. I don't mean the cover, I mean the whole seat. I bribed the maid to remove the seat from the bathroom of a Rumanian bigwig who had the room next door. That night I knocked on Mike's door and presented it to him. We have been fast friends ever since. In Havana in 1970 happiness was a warm toilet seat.

One night in the lobby, a young American sat down next to our cameraman, Keith Kay, and said, "Don't talk to me. I'm dangerous."

"I can live with that," Keith told him.

"No, really," the kid said. "I hijacked an Eastern Airlines plane and they've got me and a lot of other hijackers under house arrest a couple of blocks from the hotel."

Keith told the kid to sit tight, that he'd be right back. Then he came upstairs and told me what he had run into.

I knocked on Mike's door. It was about ten o'clock. Mike, who had been fast asleep, came to the door in his undershorts and a T-shirt. "What's up?" he said.

"Want to risk going to La Cubana Prison?" I asked.

"For what?" Mike said.

"Keith has found a hijacker who lives in a house near the hotel with a lot of other hijackers," I said.

"That," said Mike, "is worth risking La Cubana Prison for. Where's Carlos?" Carlos was the government man assigned to watch us.

"He's gone to bed," I said.

"Okay," Mike said. "Let's round up the crew and go."

As we were sneaking out of the back door of the hotel with our camera and microphones, we ran into a Swede named Goonesch Karabuda who was in Havana making a film.

"Where you going?" he asked.

"We found a hijacker," I said, "and he's going to take us to a place near the hotel where they've got several just like him under house arrest."

"You mean the skinny kid who hangs around the lobby?" he said.

"That's the one," I told him.

"He's no hijacker," Goonesch told us. "He's a deadbeat. He's told that same story to every one of us. That's how he gets us to buy him dinner and pay his bar bill."

The next night Carlos met us as we were coming out of the dining room and told us a big problem had arisen, and that all of us—Mike, me, Bill, Keith, and our soundman, Dick Wiggins—had to go with him. My first thought was that Goonesch had turned us in.

Carlos put us in a car and drove us out into the countryside. It was almost midnight when we got to an Army camp surrounded by barbed wire. We went into one of the huts.

"Wait here," Carlos said.

After about a half hour of nervously contemplating what fate awaited us, Carlos came back and said, "The colonel will see you now." We all stood up. "One at a time," Carlos said.

"Oh, oh," I thought. "It's La Cubana Prison for sure."

We went in one by one to be told by the colonel that we had overstayed our permitted time and were in the country illegally. Each of us told him the immigration people had taken our passports when we arrived, that we hadn't seen them since, and that Carlos never told us how long we could stay. Then the colonel called us all back in as a group and said, "You're right. Carlos is wrong and owes you an apology."

That's how we didn't get to go to La Cubana Prison. Incidentally, we didn't get to see Castro either.

KING:
I'll be honest with you. I can go on a court against a fellow and even if I beat him, I don't want to. Because, I'll tell you, some fellows have such a bad ego trip that it's not worth it.

DAYAN:
Things are happening . . . not the way the beginners of the Zionist movement thought they would . . . They thought we would come to a country where nobody is here—they didn't realize that many Arabs were here—and they thought everybody will be happy because we will bring money and prosperity and development and all the Jews will be nice people and they will become farmers . . . an ideal picture. Well, it didn't work out that way. It didn't work out that way.

JANET FLANNER
April 22, 1973

MIKE WALLACE:
Janet Flanner is a journalist. She has written, from Paris, for *The New Yorker* magazine for almost half a century, ever since she left Indianapolis in the early twenties . . . The high point for Americans in Paris [then] was the arrival one chilly night of Charles Lindbergh . . .

FLANNER:
All of Paris seemed to be shouting . . . "The American has arrived, the American has arrived." And it was terribly exciting because the world seemed to have been retained within the comprehension of one man's control over it. I mean, it shrank the world to the size of a thimble. And it was so touching. He leaned out of his little plane and produced his passport and said, "I am Charles Lindbergh, an American. I've just flown across the Atlantic Ocean." . . . As if they didn't expect him. Well, he didn't think they did.

MIKE WALLACE:
Look, explain something to me, will you, Mr. Ehrlichman? Why would anybody in the Nixon Administration . . . want to raise money to defend the guys who burglarized the Watergate?

EHRLICHMAN:
Certainly for no reason of self-interest . . . There may have been a compassionate motive.

WALLACE:
Compassionate!

EHRLICHMAN:
But in terms of self-interest, protecting one's own . . . that's a question that comes back to this whole cover-up thing. Cover up what? The White House had no interest, as such, in covering this thing up.

MIKE WALLACE:
Mailer's first effort at biography [is] a book about Marilyn Monroe . . . You don't believe she was murdered, really?

MAILER:
To give a handicapper's estimate, I'd say it was ten to one it was an accidental suicide. But I would not ignore the possibility of murder.

WALLACE:
Do you believe Bobby Kennedy had been with her that night?

MAILER:
I don't know.

WALLACE:
Handicap it.

MAILER:
I'd say it's even money.

MIKE WALLACE:
You're chief of staff in the [Nixon] White House. Let's say that tomorrow you learned that . . . somebody . . . had been hired by one of your subordinates to check up on the drinking habits and sexual habits, if you will, of a political opponent.

HAIG:
Well, I don't think that's the kind of thing that I'd tolerate.

WALLACE:
You'd fire him?

HAIG:
I don't think that's appropriate business for the White House.

MORLEY SAFER:

The Watergate drama has thrown up to the American audience a whole cast of characters who only a few months ago were either unknown or known only to a few Washington insiders. Well, tonight we profile one of them: Senator Daniel K. Inouye [of Hawaii]. On the battlefields of Italy, Inouye was raised from private to sergeant to lieutenant. Days before the war ended, a grenade blew away his right arm. He was sent home, and before presenting himself to his family, he stopped off for a haircut in California.

INOUYE:

I was in an officer's uniform, I had four rows of ribbons—a big bona fide hero. So I walked in, and one barber approached me and he says, "What are you?" I said, "What am I? I need a haircut." He said, "You're a Jap?" I said, "No, I'm an American." He said, "But you're a Jap." I said, "Well, if you mean what my parents were . . . yeah, my father was born in Japan." [He said,] "We don't cut Jap hair here!"

MORLEY SAFER:
Is chasing girls easier now that you're *the* Woody Allen?

ALLEN:
Some situations become a little easier when you're known because you can approach people more easily and they know you're not going to do something terrible to them—and they're wrong.

JOHN MAHER
January 27, 1974

MORLEY SAFER:

John Maher . . . runs a center for misfits . . . right in the heart of San Francisco's smartest neighborhood . . . [They're] criminals who have decided to heal each other—many of them drug addicts.

MAHER:

What we have here is a sane asylum. You see, years ago, when only a few people were crazy, you used to have insane asylums . . . Now, when it seems like everybody is crazy, what we had to do was start a sane asylum for ourselves . . . and for a couple of years deal with each other sanely . . . One of the things guys like us got to break is the bind between right-wing nuts who want to beat everybody on the head and poor weak-kneed, bleeding heart, vicarious thrill, radical chic creepos who want to kiss your backside.

ERIC SEVAREID:
This country's about the only one in the world I know of where people have made it almost a sin to grow old . . . Now there's a new movement somebody started . . . to liberate the old.

MRS. LONGWORTH:
Is there really? That is fun!

SEVAREID:
To make people understand that old people have feelings, that they even have sexual passion . . . Are you all for that?

MRS. LONGWORTH:
Well, as long as they don't do it in the streets.

"PRINCESS ALICE AT 90"

She lived in one of those old turn-of-the century mansions on Massachusetts Avenue that looked like it had seen better days. Eric Sevareid had run into her at a party and had the feeling she could be talked into an appearance on *60 Minutes.* Although, several years before, we had been permitted by the lady to run parts of an interview she had done for British Television, the chance to get Alice Roosevelt Longworth, Teddy Roosevelt's legendary daughter, to do an exclusive interview for *60 Minutes* was just too delicious to pass up. Alice Roosevelt at ninety! That was the kind of story we were in business to do. I called her. She invited me to tea. Should I bring a gift? Maybe I should send something. Why not a television set?

"Why not a television set?" My secretary, Suzanne Davis, was scornful. "Because it would be *gauche,* that's why not."

After conferring with Maxine Cheshire, who wrote social items for the Washington *Post* and knew from *gauche,* I decided to bring her a plant. "She likes those little Japanese dwarf trees," Maxine told me.

After I gave her the plant I told her I had almost committed a *faux pas* by sending her a television set, but luckily my secretary had warned me that it would be *gauche.*

"What's *gauche* about a television set?" Mrs. Longworth asked. The next day we sent her a large color television set, but she called to complain that it wasn't large enough. We got her a bigger one.

With the set ensconced in her house, we set a date for the interview, but when we arrived we were told by the woman who opened the door that she was still in bed and had no intention of coming downstairs for *60 Minutes,* Eric Sevareid or God. At that point I heard a voice from upstairs:

"Is that you, Mr. Hewitt?"

"It's me, Mrs. Longworth. How you doing?"

"I'm doing terrible and I'm not going to do your interview."

"Come on, Mrs. Longworth, what's the matter with you?"

"Nothing's the matter with me. I'm an old lady and I don't have to do anything I don't want to do. So get out of my house."

"Mrs. Longworth, what am I going to tell Mr. Sevareid?"

"Tell him I don't like him and I don't like you and I don't like *60 Seconds.*"

About that time, her companion arrived at the bottom of the stairs, whispered to me to go into the parlor, set up the cameras and wait. Everything, she assured me, would be all right. A half hour later Mrs. Longworth appeared as if nothing had happened and was warm, delightful and couldn't have been more fun. After we finished the interview I noticed an embroidered pillow on her couch that said: IF YOU CAN'T SAY SOMETHING NICE ABOUT SOMEONE, COME SIT BY ME. That gave me the opening. "You know, don't you, that you scared the hell out of me this morning?"

"Didn't I now?" she said, twinkling with impish delight.

THE GENTLEMEN FROM CBS

Alice Roosevelt Longworth was of a certain age and a certain era when "ladies" and "gentlemen" were still in vogue. It was the era when, after something or other had happened at the Vanderbilt mansion and the press descended on the house, the butler, so the story goes, told Mrs. Vanderbilt, "Madam, there are several reporters at the door and a gentleman from the *Herald*."

That's how I felt about CBS News in the 1950s and early 1960s. There were several reporters and the gentlemen from CBS—Edward R. Murrow, Eric Sevareid, Howard K. Smith, Charles Collingwood, Winston Burdette, Alexander Kendrick, Richard C. Hottelet, Bill Downs, Larry Le Seur, Martin Agronsky and David Schoenbrun. They were the best in the world.

The one I was the closest to was Schoenbrun, the ex-GI, ex-schoolteacher, who was picked by Murrow right after the war to be our man in Paris. Right now, he's not our man anywhere. Although he was, pound for pound, as good a reporter as I have ever known, pound for pound he sank under the weight of his own mishegoss—foolishness, for those who don't know. Also for those who don't know, the signoff "David Schoenbrun, CBS News, Paris" was as much a trademark of CBS radio's early morning *World News Roundup* as, later, Cronkite's "And that's the way it is" was of CBS television's Evening News.

No matter. As we moved into the television age, David became convinced that everyone at CBS was out to get him, which they weren't, but one day someone at CBS did—David, himself. Not long after he left Paris to become our Washington bureau chief, he got sacked. His version of why it happened and CBS's version don't square with each other, but suffice it to say that CBS's version was not unrelated to mishegoss like this: When my then fiancée, Frankie Childers, told President Kennedy she was going to marry someone at CBS, the President asked, "Is he a pygmy?"

"A pygmy?" she asked. "What do you mean, 'Is he a pygmy?'"

"I don't know," the President said. "Schoenbrun says that over at CBS he's surrounded by pygmies."

David, you silly son-of-a-bitch, you had so much going for you at CBS and you were the only one who didn't know it.

For a time after Schoenbrun, Martin Agronsky was our Paris correspondent. Once several years ago when I was in his town on one of those flying visits I made from time to time to our foreign bureaus, Agronsky invited me to go with him to a dinner party. The hostess, as I recall, was not overjoyed that Martin had brought along a clod who spoke little or no French and understood even less. This crowd was none too big on Americans to start with, but, lucky for me, the attractive woman on my left at dinner was one of the few they were big on. She spoke excellent French and was, I supposed, a student.

As the evening wore on and the wine wore on, I decided to make a play for her.

What better way to impress a young American all alone in Paris than to share with her some of the wisdom this worldly wise newsman had picked up on his several trips abroad?

I was going great guns explaining to her the whys and wherefores of the low state of relations between Kennedy and De Gaulle when the waiter slipped me a note with the following from Agronsky: "Thought you'd like to know that girl you're snowing is the American Ambassador's daughter." Talk about putting your *pied* in your *bouche*. I'd like to think that Chip Bohlen's daughter never thought about that evening again. I wish I could say the same.

"Murrow's boys" were a breed apart, and so was Ed. His favorite story was one he told about himself. It seemed that he and Moshe Dayan were in a jeep driving to an airstrip in the Negev so Murrow could catch a plane back to Tel Aviv en route home. As Murrow told it: Dayan said, "You know, Murrow, the whole free world owes you a debt for the broadcasts you did during World War II." To which Ed said he replied: "Oh, General, I wasn't the only one. There was Elmer Davis and a lot of others who were just as good, maybe better."

Murrow said Dayan was quiet for another mile or so of desert road and then said: "I never saw a television broadcast as good as the one you did on Joe McCarthy." To which Murrow replied, "It wasn't me. It was Fred Friendly and Joe Wershba and Eddie Scott and Palmer Williams and a lot of other guys."

Again Dayan lapsed into silence. A few miles later he said, "Okay, but your Christmas in Korea documentary was a classic." "Can't take credit for that either, General," Murrow said. "That was the product of a lot of great cameramen like Charlie Mack and Marty Barnett and Leo Rossi and Bill McClure."

Then, Murrow said, Dayan shut up until they got to the airstrip. They shook

MURROW IS THE ONE WEARING A TIE

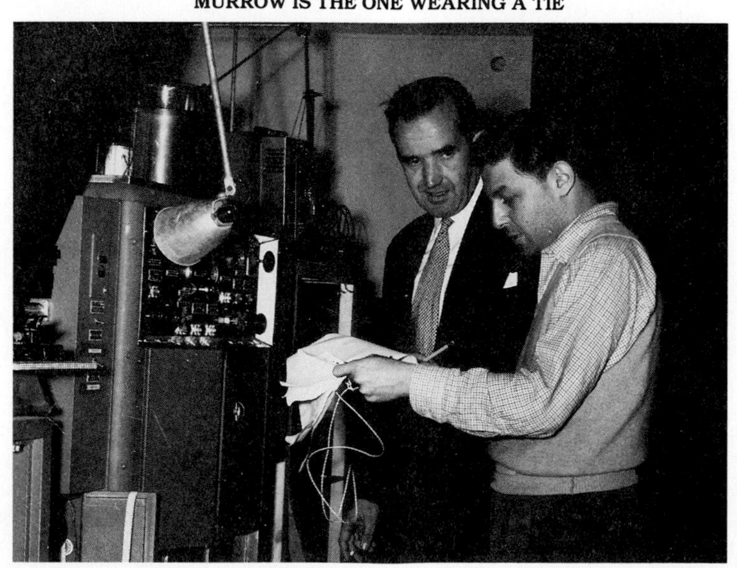

hands at the bottom of the steps and just as Murrow was about to disappear through the door of the plane, Dayan shouted up the steps: "Murrow?" "Yes, sir." "Don't be so modest. You're not that good."

The truth is that they were all "that good" and there will never again be a staff of reporters like them.

Better Late than Never

One summer night in 1956 when I heard on my car radio that the ocean liners *Andrea Doria* and *Stockholm* had collided in a fog bank off Nantucket, I immediately went to a phone booth and called Doug Edwards—who was brought up in the Murrow tradition. I then called the CBS news desk and told them to have a film crew meet us at the Naval Air Station at Quonset Point, Rhode Island. Doug Edwards and I were on our way. But we got there late, and when we pulled up at the Naval Air Station all the other cameramen and reporters were already heading back to their newspapers and radio and television stations with the story. We still wanted to fly over the site of the abandoned *Andrea Doria*. I hated not to be first, but at least we could get an eyewitness account of the big liner wallowing in the sea. A Navy pilot took pity on us and said he'd fly us out to the site even though the regular press flight had been there almost an hour before. Twenty minutes or so later we were airborne.

As we approached the wreck, we opened the door of the chopper and Doug stood in the opening so we could film him in the foreground with the ship below us.

"How long do you think she'll stay afloat?" I asked the pilot, figuring he would say "a few days, maybe a week."

"Don't stop that camera," he said. "She looks like she's going down."

DOUG EDWARDS AND YOURS TRULY LOOKING LIKE TWO CHARACTERS OUT OF "HAPPY DAYS"

And sure enough, with our camera grinding away and Doug looking down and describing it, the *Andrea Doria* rolled over like a big dead elephant, and as the water emptied out of its swimming pools, she sank. I couldn't quite believe I had seen what I had seen. One minute she was there and the next she was gone. When we landed we called the news desk. "Tough luck," the editor said. "Everybody else has already been on the air with pictures of the ship. The only thing we can do now is go back in a few days and catch it as she sinks."

"She already has," I said, "and Doug and I have it all on film."

In 1962, Walter Cronkite replaced Doug Edwards on the evening news. It wasn't that Doug wasn't first rate, it was that Cronkite was irresistible. He had "anchorman" written all over his face. The CBS brass only had to take one look at this former United Press war correspondent and they were ready to make a major commitment to television news. They seemed happy to have me aboard as his sidekick. At least. the people in charge before Friendly were happy to have me aboard.

"Go, Baby, Go!"

Nobody ever said it because nobody had to say it, and if they had, it would have been embarrassing to both television and NASA, America's space agency. I always figured there was an understanding between television and NASA—never spelled out, never even whispered, never even hinted at, but they knew and we knew. If we continued to provide first-class coverage of the space race, they would in turn give us, free of charge, the most spectacular television shows anyone had even seen. Those of us who produced the television coverage of space soon found out that what we were getting was a lot more than free television shows. What we were getting as well was a chance to show the American people that we were team players,

AND THAT'S THE WAY IT WAS . . .

and that if television brought you distasteful things like race riots and a war we couldn't win, it also brought you the astronauts. It was a chance for television to show that it, too, had the right stuff.

There was no practitioner of the art better than Cronkite, who was known during those first manned flights as "the eighth astronaut." Nobody seemed to mind that at times he was their cheerleader. "Go, baby, go!" The public loved it. When John Glenn's mother first came to Cape Canaveral and was asked what she wanted to see, she said, "Walter Cronkite." During the weeks leading up to each space shot we all hung out at the Holiday Inn in Cocoa Beach, we and our kids and the astronauts and their kids. Nobody was impressed with anybody except maybe with Scott Crossfield and Chuck Yeager when they flew into town from their test pilot base in California.

As for the astronauts, you really can't be impressed with a guy when your kid and his kid pee in the same pool. Although they didn't live at the Holiday Inn, that's where they hung out and sometimes dropped in for breakfast on their way out to where they were gearing up for a launch. They may have been the first American heroes we'd had in a long time—Shepard, Grissom, Glenn, Schirra, Cooper, Carpenter and Slayton—but they were also the guys you had bacon and eggs with in the morning.

Did they mind us hanging around? I don't think so. We kind of went with the territory. The Air Force officer who was assigned to look after them, Colonel John E. "Shorty" Powers, managed to get his face on television more often than the astronauts. Once, during one of those interminable weather delays, a couple of us decided we'd had enough of Cocoa Beach and would drive to Miami. We ended up in a joint called the Bonfire on one of the causeways separating Miami Beach from Miami proper. Shorty, who fancied himself something of a ladies' man (didn't we all?), turned to a wicked-looking brunette sitting next to him at the bar (every Miami Beach

BLASTING OFF WITH CRONKITE AND WALLY SCHIRRA

brunette sitting at a bar looked wicked to me) and introduced himself. "I'm Colonel John E. Powers; I'm in charge of the astronauts." She looked back and introduced herself. "Fifty bucks," she said.

There was also the time when Bob Wussler, who later became president of CBS Television, and I were producing the CBS space coverage, and we got a call from New York telling us that Arthur Godfrey was coming down to the Cape and to please arrange to take care of him. That Saturday night, Godfrey, Cronkite and I were at a table watching the show at the Starlite when a leggy redhead, a new girl in town, walked in and decided, without anyone asking her, to squeeze in between Godfrey, America's best-known radio personality, and Cronkite, America's eighth astronaut. I noticed the maître d', or what passed for a maître d' at the Starlite Motel, trying to catch my eye. "You better tell Cronkite and Godfrey to watch out," he said. "Her husband is a mobster and he couldn't care less who they are."

I went and found Wussler. "My God," I said, "we promised we'd take care of Godfrey. What if we wake up tomorrow morning and find him and Cronkite floating face down in the pool?"

"Boy, will we get hollered at," the future president of CBS Television said, and went back to his drink.

Cronkite, as everyone knows, was still right side up when the next bunch of astronauts came along. They were the ones heading for the moon, and one night at a NASA cocktail party for them Cronkite ran into Charles Lindbergh and got into a conversation about Lindbergh's son, with whom Cronkite had done some filming and of whom he was very fond. Lindbergh, like any proud father, asked Cronkite if he could introduce him to his wife so she could hear the wonderful things Walter was saying about their son. Walter said he had always wanted to meet Anne Morrow Lindbergh. They crossed the room and when they got a few steps away from Anne Lindbergh, Charles A. Lindbergh turned to Walter Cronkite and said, "Excuse me, but what did you say your name was?" Lindbergh, it turned out, never watched television.

Although Cronkite and I have been pretty close over the years, we've had our occasional run-ins. Betsy Cronkite, on the other hand, is the living end. If there was a sweetheart of Sigma Chi, Betsy is the sweetheart of CBS. She giggles a lot and everybody loves her, and has a favorite "Betsy" story. There's the one about the time Walter called out from the bathroom, where he was shaving, "Betsy, phone '21' and get a table. I feel like going out."

A moment or two later Betsy told Walter, "I called. They don't have any tables. They're fully booked."

"Christ, Betsy," he said. "Call them back and tell them who you are." ("That's what Walter calls me," she said once, "Christ, Betsy.") Dutiful wife that she was, she called them back and said, "I'm Betsy Cronkite," and hung up.

"What the hell are you doing, Betsy!" Walter exclaimed.

"I did what you told me to," she said. "I called them and told them who I was."

When Walter brought Betsy down to Cocoa Beach, we usually had fun, but mostly we sat around figuring out how not to go stir crazy. And if you saw the movie *The Right Stuff*, you know some of the astronaut wives had the same trouble. The trick was not to get yourself too revved before a launch because it was an even-money bet it would be delayed. That's when you had to think up things to keep yourself amused, like the time a CBS stage manager named Snooks O'Brien arrived for his first visit to the Cape and Al Thaler, one of our unit managers, told him that the most beautiful sight he would ever see in his life was the early morning launch of the test rocket. He pointed it out to Snooks and told him it usually went up between six and seven and not to take his eyes off it or he would miss the spectacular colors that surrounded it during the first few seconds as it left the pad. Snooks was enthralled, and for more than half an hour he peered at the towering missile a mile or so away on the horizon. It was not quite 7:00 A.M. when someone passed by and asked him what he was looking at. He said he was waiting for the early morning test rocket to go up.

"Where?" the other guy asked.

"Over there," Snooks answered.

"Over there?" said the other guy. "That's not a rocket. That's the Cape Canaveral Lighthouse."

It was just before John Glenn's flight that I noticed that what we were missing from our coverage was any sense of a shared experience. Wouldn't it be good, I thought, if we could make every viewer feel he was truly part of the day's excitement? That's when I got the idea of putting a large television screen in Grand Central Station, where I knew it would draw a crowd. I also knew that by putting cameras in Grand Central, we could show the viewers at home that a lot of others were watching the same thing they were at the same time. What I didn't know was just how big a crowd we would draw. During Glenn's re-entry into the earth's atmosphere—those minutes when the earth stations lost contact with him and no one knew whether he was dead or alive—the crowd in Grand Central swelled to thousands. The cheer that went up when Cronkite said Glenn was safe and sound and back from space was deafening. It was just what I was after, and I'll bet some of the people watching all alone in their own living rooms joined in too when the crowd cheered. I told you we had "the right stuff."

The Brass

In those days my immediate boss was the late Paul Levitan, who had the title Director of Special Events and who was in charge of our space coverage. His talent for murdering the English language was almost as legendary around CBS as Murrow's and Sevareid's talent for using it properly. Paul was responsible for some of the most incredible statements anyone ever heard.

In critiquing the pilot of a show with Walter Cronkite and Jack Paar, he said,

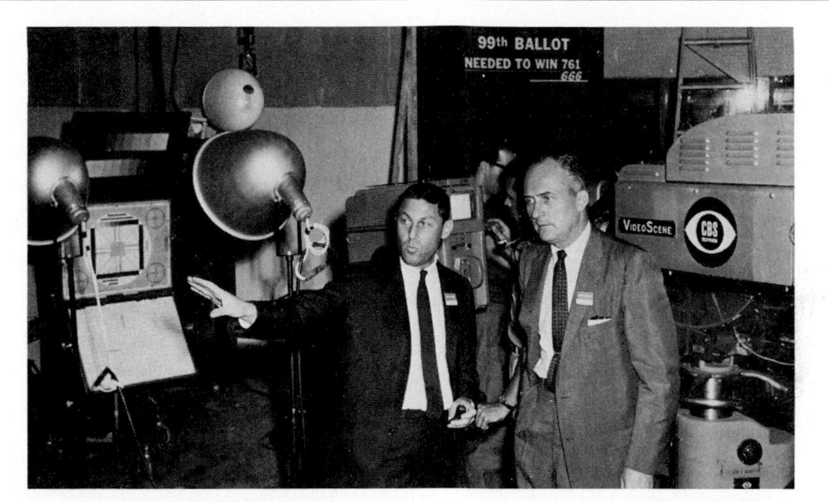

I HAVE NO IDEA WHAT SIG MICKELSON AND I WERE DOING EXCEPT MAYBE POSING FOR A PICTURE

"The trouble with this show is that it has no semblance." Everybody left the room guffawing except me. I thought, Jesus, he's hit it on the head. That's exactly what this show lacks, semblance.

In describing the control room setup for the 1956 Democratic Convention, he said, "Hewitt will sit in the middle. At one elbow will be John Day, and at the other elbow will be Mac Johnson, and I will be at his other elbow."

Paul's all-time greatest—even better than the time he told me a lot of water had run under the dam—was when he was asked why he was bringing so many cameramen and soundmen to Ike's second inauguration. He said, honest to God, "We want everyone we can get. We don't want to lose the dike for want of an extra finger."

I've had a lot of bosses. During my thirty-seven years at CBS, seven men have run the News division. My favorite was Bill Leonard, who came up through the ranks. He and I were cut from the same piece of cloth and he was a good friend. So was Sig Mickelson, who, in the early days, encouraged me to try new things, and Dick Salant, under whom we started *60 Minutes,* although it was a tough sell.

Sig Mickelson says it was he who coined the title "anchorman," at the 1952 Republican Convention. I thought I had, but Sig could be right. At any rate, we both had a hand in it. In trying to explain what Cronkite's role would be vis-à-vis our other reporters, I said they would be a team—a relay team, if you will, and Sig, as best I remember, said Cronkite would run the final leg, the anchor leg. It had nothing to do with being "anchored" to a desk or "anchored" to anything, but it has come into such common usage that an "anchorman" who also goes on location is known today as a "floating anchor." And you can't get much sillier than that. An "anchor" is really a dumb thing to call Dan Rather or Tom Brokaw or Peter Jennings. But it's too late. It's part of the language.

Although Salant, who followed Mickelson, had been a lawyer, and a damned good one, his heart was in journalism and his mission in life was to protect journalists from lawyers and legislators who were trying to nibble away at the First Amendment. His reputation in this area was so well known that when Leonard succeeded him as president of the News Division, he said (in his first speech to the CBS affiliates) that he hoped to take up where Salant left off and quote to them from the First Amendment—but when he went looking for it, he couldn't find it. Salant had taken it with him when he left.

Mickelson, Salant and Leonard were right out of the Bill Paley–Frank Stanton school of broadcasting that said: Whatever you do, do it with style. Although Paley happily stayed on past retirement age, the two of them, chairman and president, were such a powerful team, such a 1–2 punch, that I thought there was a chance we might not survive Stanton's leaving. For a while we almost didn't, almost went into the tank, until Paley fished a young vice president named Gene Jankowski out of the executive pool and put him in charge of the broadcast group. I always figured Paley believed a lot of Frank Stanton had rubbed off on Gene Jankowski, just as I like to believe a lot of Mickelson, Salant and Leonard rubbed off on me.

As I made clear earlier, Fred Friendly's reign wasn't the happiest time for me. Nothing about either of us rubbed off on the other. The problem was that he didn't really approve of me. After all, Fred was not the kind of man who would sully himself brawling with another network. He was the kind of man who would hold your coat while you did. ("You hit 'em, kid. I'll be around the corner looking out for the cops.")

For instance, at Winston Churchill's funeral, I tricked the Royal Canadian Air Force into holding up a military flight, the one that was carrying NBC's videotape of the ceremony. At that time the satellite over the Atlantic operated only during certain hours, so all three networks had to supplement what they had transmitted via satellite with videotape shipped by jet. To get almost an hour's jump on the competition, I arranged to videotape the BBC's output at Dublin Airport, where we had a chartered Pan Am 707 standing by to take off at our command. When NBC got wind of what we were doing, they arranged to share an RCAF flight from London with the Canadian Broadcasting System. That flight, which was going solely to carry the NBC and CBC tape, was standing by to take off on command from the CBC, and if it took off before our Dublin flight, the faster military jet would beat us back across the Atlantic.

There had to be a way around this one. There was. First I had to get the phone number of the RCAF operations shack at the London airport, which wasn't too tough. Then, I got on two phones near a window, where I could watch the RCAF jet on the tarmac through a pair of binoculars. On one phone I had Art Kane and Dick Sedia, our two guys in Dublin; on the other I had the RCAF operations officer. Luckily, he had only one number and I had it tied up. Naturally, I did nothing to correct his impression that he was talking to the CBC. After all, it's very easy to confuse CBC with CBS. To the RCAF officer I kept shouting, "Don't take off. There's more videotape on the way." Meanwhile, I told Kane and Sedia to let me know when the 707 took off. Finally, the word came: "Wait five minutes for us to be airborne and then let the

JFK, DH, AND FF

RCAF plane go. They'll never catch us." Five minutes later I gave the RCAF the word that no more tape was coming and that they should leave.

Of course, we won the race, but when the CBC finally got through on the RCAF phone I had had tied up for almost an hour, they were furious about the delay and even more furious when they were told one of their own men had asked for it. I guess I shouldn't have been surprised that the next person they called was me. "Did you call the RCAF and tell them you were the CBC?" an angry voice demanded.

"I'll look into it and call you back," I said.

Friendly was delighted that our tape got on the air first. Did he know how we had done it? I don't know, but he does now.

My favorite story about Friendly is one he tells about teaching at the Columbia University School of Journalism. The first day he showed up, one of his students came to class wearing a button that said MAKE LOVE, NOT WAR.

Fred said to her, "I don't think that's an appropriate button to wear to class."

"Oh, Mr. Friendly," she said, "you're so square you think making love is making out."

Friendly says that that day at lunch he told Walter Lippmann about the student who had told him "you're so square you think making love is making out," to which Lippmann replied, "What the hell is making out?"

The next day he told his class he'd had lunch with Walter Lippmann, who asked him, "What the hell is making out?" Friendly thought that pretty well summed up the generation gap until a student got up and said, "Who the hell is Walter Lippmann?"

I always thought nobody could top that until I told the story to a group of journalism students. When I got to the punch line, "Who the hell is Walter Lippmann," one of them stood up and said, "Who the hell is Fred Friendly?"

Friendly always liked to have people "on call." Sometimes he even put himself "on call." One rainy Sunday afternoon in 1964, he and I were sitting in the newsroom watching NBC take us apart on the Alaskan earthquake story. Early in the evening, when it became apparent that our troops were not going to get there in time to save the day, we decided to pack it in, go home, lick our wounds and regroup to fight another day. Our effort had registered zero on the Richter scale. As the two of us straggled out into the rain, he asked me if he could give me a lift home. That was okay by me. I hoped we could talk about his canning me off the Cronkite News, but he didn't have anything to say about that or anything else as he drove me home.

Now, when Fred Friendly is dejected he looks like a parade float losing helium. As he slumped behind the wheel, the windshield wipers punctuating the silence—clunk, clunk, clunk—I could feel it coming. You could always feel it coming. Friendly, who never left an analogy unturned, was about to say something portentous, and he did. The president of CBS News said in his best never-leave-an-analogy-unturned voice, "The Alaska earthquake is my Bay of Pigs." Holy shit, I thought, this guy really believes that. (For those of you too young to remember, the Bay of Pigs was a debacle that befell another President. His name was John F. Kennedy.)

Prevailing opinion has it that Friendly's most noteworthy accomplishment was bringing Edward R. Murrow into television—but not to me. To me, his most noteworthy accomplishment was bringing Palmer Williams into television. Palmer was second in command around *60 Minutes* through all our growing years and most of our glory years. He was the navigator without whom we never would have picked our way through the minefield that had, up until 1968, sunk every other broadcast of our kind. You name it, Palmer can tell you about it . . . General Motors, General Eisenhower, General Sarnoff, airline schedules, television cameras, GNP as well as who played what part in a 1930s Broadway musical. Today, retired, he is a *60 Minutes* consultant, and just the sight of him in the halls reassures me that if we keep doing things Palmer's way, we might just have a few more glory years in us.

CALLAS:
A woman has to learn to say no. Otherwise she won't be a lady, not a lady.

MIKE WALLACE:
Have you said no enough, Madame Callas?

CALLAS:
Oh, never enough, but not bad.

WALLACE:
Have you said yes enough?

CALLAS:
You don't have to say yes.

MIKE WALLACE:
When you were a little boy you saw visions, you saw apparitions. God came to you, or God's messenger came to you?

SHAH:
Yes . . . Sometimes I have dreams which come true, and I don't like it . . . When I was a kid, once I dreamed that there was a pit full of snakes. And people who are always translating the dreams told me that these were my enemies, things like that.

WALLACE:
You know, very few leaders . . . talk with the candor with which you have talked on television. Why? Why are you willing to?

SHAH:
. . . Because this confidence exists between me and my people. They trust in me; I trust in them.

THE KISSINGER CONNECTION

After the Shah was deposed, we did a story on *60 Minutes* called "The Kissinger-Shah Connection." Dan Rather was the reporter, and to say Kissinger wasn't happy wouldn't say half of it.

When we told him we wanted to interview him for it, one day he'd say okay, we could interview him, and the next day he'd call and say he'd changed his mind. The interview was on and off so many times that we postponed the story a week waiting for him to make up his mind. But when push came to shove he not only decided not to do the interview, but tried every which way to get us to call off the story. When he wasn't telling me that Dan Rather was out to get him, he was telling Dan that I was out to get him.

My wife, Marilyn Berger, had covered Kissinger when she was the diplomatic correspondent for the Washington *Post,* and had been on his plane shuttling between Jerusalem, Damascus, Amman, Cairo and Riyadh while he was trying to put together a Middle East peace package. On the Monday after *60 Minutes* ran "The Kissinger-Shah Connection," Marilyn and I had dinner at the Kissingers' (the invitation had been issued before they knew about the *60 Minutes* story).

Even though everything was cordial at dinner, the next morning, two days after the show had been on the air, Henry's friends were still calling to say we had defamed him (Henry's friends think anything that's not a paean of praise is defamatory). So, I decided to write him a letter: "Dear Henry: You may have been a great Secretary of State, but you are not the Statue of Liberty or the Washington Monument, and I think it's unrealistic of you to expect us to treat you like a national shrine." I then went on to say, "You have been ill-advised if you think you can dictate that history's view of [the Kissinger] years will be seen solely through your eyes. It doesn't work that way. It didn't for Abe Lincoln, George Washington, Franklin Roosevelt or Dwight Eisenhower. A little criticism goes with the territory. Even Jack Dempsey took one on the chin from time to time. It's easier when you roll with the punches."

The next time I saw Henry, I said, "Did you get my letter?"

"I got it," he said.

"And . . . ?"

"I got it."

HELEN GURLEY BROWN
March 31, 1974

MORLEY SAFER:

Women's Liberationists . . . accuse Mrs. Brown of perpetrating the masculine idea that women are nothing but sex objects. Mrs. Brown's answer is that being a sex object is and should be the main concern of women. And she lets it all hang out every month in *Cosmopolitan* magazine.

BROWN:

I feel being a sex object is so divine and so wonderful that there is nothing better; that you can be a sex object and you can also be the president of General Motors. I think men are sex objects. And it certainly doesn't slow you down—that women desire you sexually. You're still able to get on with your work every day.

SAFER:

I wouldn't . . . if every day I did what *Cosmo* expected of me.

MORLEY SAFER:
Do you regret that you haven't gotten married and had children and raised—

NUREYEV:
No!

SAFER:
—small Nureyevs perhaps?

NUREYEV:
No, no. What if they were not as good as me? What would I do with those imbeciles?

MORLEY SAFER:
The next time you run into someone who is different, you might do well to remember the story you are about to see. [It's] excerpted from a film by Lord Snowdon and Derek Hart, called *Born To Be Small.*

SMALL WOMAN:
One of the things about being small is that you're more or less in a little world of your own. It's very difficult to make friends, but it's even harder to keep them. You go out and you meet people who think, oh, isn't she sweet.

"BORN TO BE SMALL"

Tony Snowdon or the Earl of Snowdon or Anthony Armstrong-Jones, take your choice, was as good with an Arri as he was, and still is, with a Leica. (An Arri, in case you don't know, is an Arriflex, which is a 16-millimeter movie camera; hardly anyone uses them anymore, so there's no reason why you should know.) How the Earl, one of the world's best photographers, came to put down his Leica and pick up our Arri is a story that began at London's Savoy Hotel, where I got into a cab one evening feeling more British than American, which is an affliction that hits me somewhere between saying goodbye to the Pan Am stewardess and arriving at Her Majesty's immigration counter. Anyway, there I was in the back of the cab, when the driver turned around and asked, "Where to?"

"Kensington Palace, please," I replied in my best British accent.

"You mean the Kensington Palace Hotel, don't you?" the driver asked—nicely, I'm sure, but I didn't hear it that way.

"Oh no, I don't," I said. "I mean the Kensington Palace Palace!"

That was the last exchange I had with the driver, who moved out into traffic headed for Kensington Palace secure in the knowledge that the bobby at the gate would know what to do with the upstart in the back of his cab.

But the bobby knew I was expected and waved us on. Arriving at the front door, or whatever it is that you call the entrance to a palace, I tripped over the Lady Sarah's kiddie car. Anyone named The Lady Sarah should have a coach-and-four and not a kiddie car, but that's what she had.

That's when I met Tony's wife. Tony's wife, at the time, was Her Royal Highness Princess Margaret. The Lady Sarah was their baby daughter.

At dinner I told them about my experience at the Savoy, how I had told the cab driver, "Kensington Palace."

"I know," Princess Margaret said. "Then he said 'you mean the Kensington Palace Hotel, don't you?'"

"How did you know that?" I asked, figuring she was not only a Princess but a mind reader.

"Happens to all our guests" was her answer. I thought she was going to say, "Happens to me all the time."

Before dinner was over, Tony had decided to take the Arri and play with it for a while and let me know in a week whether he wanted to dabble in cinematography. A week later he called and said he'd like to take a fling at it. I knew all along he would. He wanted, he said, to do a film about old age. I said, "Great, we'd love it."

When it came time to look at his first "rushes," Bill McClure, whom I assigned to be Tony's producer on *Don't Count the Candles,* had arranged a screening room in Soho for ten o'clock on a Saturday morning. (If London's Fleet Street belongs to the press, Soho belongs to the cinema, or at least it used to. It's where a lot of the movie companies have headquarters alongside Chinese restaurants and massage parlors as well as film labs, sound studios and screening rooms.)

Saturday morning Tony called and said he couldn't make the ten o'clock screening. "The Queen wants me to go with her to the opening of the monkey house at the zoo," he said.

"You're putting me on," I said.

"No, really," he said. "She insists."

I called McClure and told him to reschedule the screening. "Why?" he said.

"We got screwed—royally," I said.

Tony got an Emmy for *Don't Count the Candles.* His next film was not about old people, but about little people, and it was just too good not to run on *60 Minutes.*

SMALL MAN: People are inclined to regard you, when they see you for the first time, as a clown or as an acrobat. We seem to be something out of touch. You never see us . . . as solicitors, or you won't see us as judges, or you won't see us as soldiers, obviously, or you won't see us in shops or behind counters. And I understand it in a way, because I don't think there's anything more upsetting than a person going into a shop, and suddenly [he] finds himself being served by somebody like me.

I remember years ago when I . . . was about eight or nine. I was playing in the street with some friends, and we saw this funny little man walking towards us. . . . Well, we all rushed up to this funny little man and started calling him "Funny Little Man"—calling him names, you know, as children would. And my pal, one of my friends, turned around and said to me, "Look, Roy! He's just like you."

MORLEY SAFER:
Remember that phrase: "Extremism in the defense of liberty is no vice, moderation in the pursuit of justice is no virtue"? It was the slogan and the epitaph of Barry Goldwater's run for the presidency in 1964 . . . Goldwater believed in it, and so did the man who came up with it, Karl Hess, crew-cut, clean-shaven supporter of right-wing causes. . . . Well, Karl Hess today is still a true believer, but in the extreme left. He has become a nonviolent anarchist and tax resister. . . .

HESS:
The one thing I am not now nor have I ever been, is a liberal. . . . The liberal conception is that people are dumb, people are generally stupid, and that, therefore, they have to have highly educated people—a few highly educated people—run their lives for them. . . . Conservatives think all people are lazy, and therefore they require an autocratic economy to get them up in the morning, get them working and doing good things. But of those, the liberal, I think, is the worst.

MIKE WALLACE:
You held your hand over a blowtorch or a candle to impress a lady friend?

LIDDY:
That's not quite accurate. . . . However, I will tell you that I have done things like that numbers of times—not to impress lady friends; it's a training device for the will. If you look back in history, you'll find that's not unusual at all. There was a Roman king who did the same thing. He frightened off another king with the same act and gained thereafter the title of Scaevola, the Left-Handed—because he'd literally cooked his right hand away. He did what was necessary to save Rome.

"THE MAN WHO WOULDN'T TALK . . . TALKS"

The first time I met Gordon Liddy, Mike and I, along with Mike's producer, Marion Goldin, and CBS News vice president Gordon Manning, had driven out into the Washington, D.C., suburbs where Liddy was living while he was waiting to be sentenced for his part in the Watergate break-in. When we walked into his house, German martial music was playing on the hi-fi. When he arrived to greet us I'm sure he didn't say "Sieg Heil," but I think that's what I heard. If it was an act, it was a damned good one. He came on as one tough hombre. He wasn't scary looking. He was kind of unprepossessing, but he acted as if there were a place waiting for him at the table at Valhalla because he was a Viking and could do what other mortal men could not.

One of the things he was able to do that other mortal men could not was to get *60 Minutes* to pay him for an interview. It was the first and last time we did that. Just a few weeks before, Mike had interviewed Bob Haldeman and we were still taking flak for paying Haldeman, a convicted felon, $100,000 to sit down with Mike. The fact is *60 Minutes* hadn't paid Haldeman a penny. The Haldeman interviews had run on back-to-back Sundays as CBS News specials in the *60 Minutes* time slot, and because they were done by Mike, the critics assumed they were on *60 Minutes*—and ipso facto unloaded on me. No matter that the newspapers they worked for had paid for news tips and news stories long before *60 Minutes* saw the light of day; it was the amount that rankled them. The whole thing reminded me of the story told about Winston Churchill, who supposedly said to a lady at dinner, "Would you go to bed with me for a hundred pounds?" The lady replied, so the story goes, "Yes, I think I would."

"Would you for five pounds?" Churchill then reportedly said.

"What do you take me for?" the lady replied.

"We've already determined that," Churchill is said to have answered. "Now it's just a matter of price."

Is it a good idea to pay interview subjects? Generally, it's a bad idea.

Here, aside from a lot of flak about "checkbook journalism," is more of what $15,000 paid to Gordon Liddy brought us.

WALLACE: Was it duty, loyalty, patriotism to plan to kidnap anti-Republican radicals from Miami Beach, from the GOP Convention, in 1972? Was it duty, loyalty, patriotism to plan to employ call girls to entrap Democratic politicians at their convention?

LIDDY: I don't comment on those tactics. I will comment on the uses, or the absence of uses, of power. Power exists to be used. The first obligation of a—of a man in power or someone seeking power is to get himself elected.

WALLACE: Is there nothing that cannot, should not, be done in the pursuit of power?

LIDDY: It depends. . . If Watergate was as it's alleged to be, it was an intelligence-gathering operation of one group of persons who were seeking to acquire power. That's all it was. It's like brushing your teeth, Michael. It's basic . . .

WALLACE: John Dean was the man who recommended you for your job at CREEP [The Committee for the ReElection of the President]. What's your opinion of John Dean?

LIDDY: I think, in all fairness to the man, you'd have to put him right up there with Judas Iscariot.

WALLACE: Judas Iscariot? In other words, he betrayed Christ? Christ being Richard Nixon.

LIDDY: No, he being a betrayer of a person in high position.

WALLACE: And what do you think his motive was?

LIDDY: To save his ass . . .

WALLACE: Your boss at CREEP was Jeb Magruder. He describes you almost as a comic figure. A "cocky, little bantam rooster," he called you, who liked to brag about his James Bondish exploits.
Did you really threaten to kill Jeb Magruder?

LIDDY: I think that's one of the few truthful statements that Jeb Magruder has made.

I didn't think much about Gordon Liddy after that, until one day I got a phone call from John Goldman, New York Bureau Chief of the L.A. *Times*, who said, "Take a close look at the film you people made when George Wallace got shot and see if one of the people in the crowd isn't a dead ringer for Gordon Liddy, Nixon's White House plumber."

That intrigued me, so I got out the film and ran it frame by frame through a viewfinder and, by God, one of the people in the crowd at the moment Wallace was shot did look like Gordon Liddy. "Come on," I said to myself, "be sensible. That's just too crazy," but I picked up the phone and called the New York office of the FBI.

It was about six o'clock on a Friday night and the agent in charge asked me when he might come around and look at the film.

I said, "How about Monday morning?"

"Fine," he said, "Monday morning."

I hung up the phone and was putting out the lights and locking up for the night when the phone rang.

"How 'bout now?" the FBI agent said.

"Okey doke, I'll wait for you."

About half an hour later two agents arrived, looked at the film, and asked if they could have it.

"Sure, why not? It's already been on the air."

Then one of the agents, who lived in New Jersey, asked me if he could give me a lift. "No thanks," I told him, "it would be out of your way."

"Not tonight," he said. "I'm not going home. We've got a plane waiting for us at La Guardia. They want this film in the FBI lab tonight."

The urgency made me think I was onto something. I reminded them that if anything came of it, it was my story. After three days of hearing nothing, I phoned the FBI. "What gives?" I asked.

"It's not Liddy," they said.

"How do you know?" I asked.

They said they had used all kinds of special calibrating equipment and determined that the man in the picture was too small to be Liddy.

"Okay," I said, "if it's not Liddy, who is it?"

"No comment," they said.

Next I called George Wallace's press secretary, Billy Joe Camp, and told him what John Goldman had pointed out to me.

He said, "You and Mike are coming down to Montgomery next week to see the governor. Why don't you make some time before the interview to talk about this?"

When I arrived, Billy Joe had one of the top guys of the Alabama State Police with him. On his desk was every news photo they could get their hands on of the shooting incident. Billy Joe handed each of us a magnifying glass and the three of us spent the next hour or so in the governor's mansion pouring over the photos to see if the guy who looked like Liddy had shown up in any other pictures. We couldn't find him.

Was the FBI keeping something to themselves they should have shared with the rest of us? I think not. Were there people in the Alabama State Police who thought there was more to John Goldman's suspicions than they were being told? I got the feeling there were.

MORLEY SAFER:

When we went to the White House to chat with Betty Ford, we expected to find, quite honestly, a rather bland and predictable political wife. We found, instead, an open woman with a mind of her own, prepared to talk about anything. No taboos. She does not, like some might, play queen of America, but she's not too timid to admit that she's come a long way.

MRS. FORD:

I told my husband if we have to go to the White House, okay, I will go, but I'm going as myself. It's too late to change my pattern and if they don't like it, then they'll just have to throw me out.

"THE FIRST LADY"

The interview was off and on for months. Every time we set a date, Sheila Weidenfeld, Mrs. Ford's press secretary, called to say, "Not now. Maybe in a couple of weeks." What we suspected at the time later became public knowledge: The First Lady had a drinking problem. Anyway, the day finally came. Mrs. Gerald Ford would be at home at the White House to Mr. Morley Safer and Mr. Don Hewitt, and what's more, they were invited for lunch. While we were having lunch, the first lady of *60 Minutes,* our New York producer Merri Lieberthal, and *60 Minutes* director Arthur Bloom (Artie) were setting up the cameras and lights in the White House third floor solarium. When we got there, Artie even had the White House florists arranging and rearranging trees on the balcony overlooking the South Lawn.

Betty Ford was one of those marvelous First Ladies who tried hard not to let life in the White House intimidate her. Today it wasn't life in the White House that intimidated her, but lunch with us. We ate from trays in the upstairs sitting room and after lunch she went to her room to rest. For a while we weren't sure if we were ever going to see her again. One would think that for a First Lady lunch with *60 Minutes* would be small potatoes, but apparently she became unnerved. Morley and I loved her. I'm not so sure she loved us, but right on the dot she showed up in the solarium, calm, cool and ready for anything Morley might ask her.

SAFER: It's almost a rule of political life that the higher a man gets in politics, the less outspoken his wife becomes. She becomes a mouse. It seems that it's been just the opposite with Betty Ford . . . And among the things you have spoken out about is abortion, which is kind of a taboo subject for the wife of a President. It's one of those things that—

MRS. FORD: Once you're asked a question, you have to be honest [and say] exactly how you feel, and I feel very strongly that it was the best thing in the world when the Supreme Court voted to legalize abortion and, in my words, bring it out of the backwoods and put it in the hospitals, where it belonged. I thought it was a great, great decision.

SAFER: You've also talked about young people living together before they're married.

MRS. FORD: Well, they are, aren't they?

SAFER: Indeed they are. Well, what if Susan Ford came to you and said, "Mother, I'm having an affair"?

MRS. FORD: Certainly—well, I wouldn't be surprised. I think she's a perfectly normal human being, like all young girls. If she wanted to continue it, I would certainly counsel and advise her on the subject. And I'd want to know pretty much about the young man that she was planning to have the affair with—whether it was a worthwhile encounter, or whether it was going to be one of those . . . She's pretty young to start affairs.

SAFER: But nevertheless, old enough?

MRS. FORD: Oh, yes, she's a big girl.

SAFER: Would it surprise you, though? I mean, given the way you brought your kids up and the President brought them up. Would it surprise you if that happened?

MRS. FORD: No. I think there's a complete freedom among the young people now, and in some cases I'm not so sure that, perhaps, there would be less divorce.

This exchange about first daughters having affairs became such an issue that the President's press secretary, Ron Nessen, reportedly said about it: "That one question and answer could cost us the election." As it turned out, that one question and answer almost won them the election. The initial shock brought the most mail *60 Minutes* had ever gotten up to that point, but the aftershock brought a slew of campaign buttons that said: VOTE FOR BETTY'S HUSBAND.

Before Morley and I packed up and left, Sheila Weidenfeld, just a shade this side of panic and acting more like a bumblebee on Dexedrine than usual, asked if she could have a private word with me.

Oh, oh, I thought, she's going to ask me to edit out Mrs. Ford's remarks about her daughter having an affair. I knew I couldn't do that, but I liked Sheila and I liked Mrs. Ford and I didn't relish telling them it had to stay. Sheila began the way I knew she would: "I know I shouldn't tell you how to edit your story and as an ex-newswoman myself, I know it's beyond the pale to make a request like this, but . . ."

I was sure the next line would be: "She really didn't mean to say that." But to my amazement, that wasn't the problem at all. Sheila, whose father, Max Raab, had been in the Eisenhower White House, was savvy enough to know a political problem when she saw one: What Sheila was worried about was not sex in the White House, but an innocuous exchange between Morley and Mrs. Ford about gun control. That, to Sheila, was political dynamite. To me it was boiler plate. Knowing we were going to edit it out anyway, I told Sheila not to worry.

MRS. REAGAN:
Whenever somebody would say something about Ronnie that I felt was unkind and cruel and unjust and untrue, I'd go and take a long bath. And I would carry on imaginary conversations in the bathtub in which I was marvelous. I'd say all those right things that you hope you'd have the chance to say and all the right words would come to you and nobody could talk back to you. And I was—I was tremendous. By the time I finished the bath I was okay.

LOOKING FOR "POOR JIMMY'S" BODY

This is a story that never got on the air but did end up on page one in newspapers all over the country. The Miami *News* ran an eight-column banner headline that said: HOW CBS NEWS LOST A SCOOP IN HOFFA CASE AND $10,000. The Los Angeles *Herald-Examiner* also bannered: CBS RIPPED OFF! $10,000 AND HOFFA TIPSTER VANISH.

How did it happen? One day in the fall of 1975, Lewis Lapham, who was then editor of *Harper's*, called me and said that he had a reporter in his office with a great story, but because it would take him too long to get it into print he wanted to give it to me. Could he send the reporter over to see me? "Sure," I said. "What's his name?"

"Pat O'Keefe," he said.

Shortly after, Pat O'Keefe arrived at *60 Minutes* with a friend who claimed to know where we could find Jimmy Hoffa's body. The "friend" was one of the most *un*friendly men I had ever met. His name was Chuck Medlin and he said he had seen "poor Jimmy's body."

With cameras rolling, Morley Safer proceeded with the interview.

SAFER: Chuck.

MEDLIN: Yeah.

SAFER: Where is Jimmy Hoffa?

MEDLIN: Key West.

SAFER: Where precisely?

MEDLIN: Smith Shoal Light . . . That's where Hoffa is. It's a rockpile.

SAFER: Dead?

MEDLIN: Dead . . .

SAFER: Just lying there in the water?

MEDLIN: No, he's in cement . . .

SAFER: How was he killed?

MEDLIN: He was stabbed on a goddamn boat . . .

SAFER: What was your relationship with Jimmy Hoffa?

MEDLIN: . . . I was in a cell with him three years in Lewisburg [Federal Penitentiary]. And he coached me. I was a farm boy, I didn't know anything. I didn't have any way to get any money. I didn't have any education. I didn't have nothing. And Jimmy hired a few people out of Lewisburg . . . Jimmy hired his army of people to take care of business. I got out in September of '69. I had letters of recommendation on Local 515 in Chattanooga . . . As long as Jimmy was living, money or whatever I wanted was no problem. Because I carried bad news to people . . .

The bullshit that went on was that Jimmy was supposed to have met Tony Provenzano. Now, Tony Provenzano ain't nothing. He's a little dago looking for publicity. That's all. No less, no more. He kicked me on my leg one time in Lewisburg . . . and I told him "if you ever, ever put your god-

damn feet on me again, you're a dead sonofabitch, dago." Tony was always in Jimmy's face to make sure that his job in Jersey as a local president would be available. And I and Jimmy, you know, I worked in the butcher shop [in Lewisburg]. I'd give Jimmy his rubdowns and shaves and we cooked steaks on light bulbs, wherever we had to do it. And I and Jimmy would rap. And I became very close to him and still am . . . very close to him . . .

SAFER: How did you know where to look for Jimmy Hoffa's body?

MEDLIN: . . . You take the weakest point, and the weakest point to me was George.

SAFER: George . . . is what?

MEDLIN: He's a half-ass hit man for the Teamsters. Just a half-ass hit man. . . [I] put a .38 in his mouth, made him take me and show me at Smith Shoal Light where Jimmy is now. Where he's buried this minute.

SAFER: You went out by rowboat, right? And what did you see?

MEDLIN: The thing's there with chain around it and concrete and it's Jimmy. I can come in here with a bunch of bullshit, wouldn't be no good. I'm just telling you facts as I know how to tell them . . . I have no other God before me but Jimmy Hoffa. No other God . . .

SAFER: Will you show us where Jimmy Hoffa is buried?

MEDLIN: I said I would. If I say I will, I will.

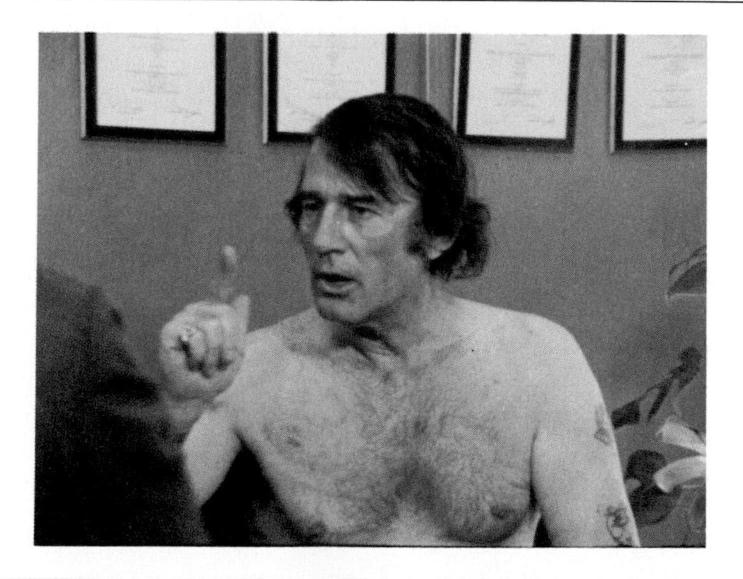

Medlin told us he wanted to talk because he had had a falling out with other Teamsters who wanted "Jimmy out of the way." Then he told me and everyone within earshot that he would kill us all if we ever told the Teamsters about his coming to see us. He said, "All I want, now, and this includes your secretaries, is to keep your mouth shut. Because if you don't, and they miss me, I'll come looking for you. And you don't want me knocking at your door. I swear, you don't want me knocking at your door. That's a promise. That's not a threat."

I don't know if I was too afraid to think clearly, but God help me, I fell hook, line and sinker for Medlin's cock-and-bull tale. Next he informed us that we would have to pay O'Keefe for the story. "Can do," I said, "but only if O'Keefe takes Morley and his producer, Joe Wershba, to the site of Hoffa's grave." What O'Keefe wanted was $10,000 in cash, which I told him I would give to Wershba to give him when Wershba and Safer had seen Hoffa's body. That's when I went to see Dick Salant, then president of CBS News, to fill him in. I guess we all had lost our marbles. Salant arranged for me to get ten one thousand dollar bills to give to Wershba to carry to Key West. But Wershba refused to take the money. "Hell, no. I'm not carrying all that cash." That's when I made my biggest mistake. I gave the money to O'Keefe, after he assured me that he would return the money if Morley and Joe were not satisfied that the body was Hoffa's. Looking back, I don't believe I did it.

O'Keefe left with the dough. Morley and Joe were to meet O'Keefe and Medlin in Key West the next day. But before Safer and Wershba had even left New York, the shit hit the fan.

O'Keefe, scared stiff of Medlin, wasn't about to make a fuss when Medlin asked for the money. They had gotten as far south as Tennessee when O'Keefe called a friend on *The New York Times* and told him the whole story, including the part about Medlin skipping with our dough.

Slowly but surely we were able to piece together the scam we had fallen victim to . . . a scam that O'Keefe, as far as I could figure out, was not part of.

The first thing I did was to call the New York City Police. Two cops from the Midtown North Precinct arrived in my office looking like two cops from *Barney Miller.*

"First of all, we have to determine," they said, "whether a crime was perpetrated within the limits of the City of New York."

"Yes," I said. "As far as I know, Medlin took some of the money from O'Keefe at gunpoint in a Manhattan hotel."

"Very good," said the cop. "Crime was perpetrated within the limits of the City of New York." What was the address of the hotel? they asked. I told them it was on West 44th Street.

"Oh, oh," they said, "that's Midtown South." And with that they up and left.

Next, two guys from the FBI arrived. They were also right out of central casting. They spent over an hour in my office, and as I escorted them to the front door they told me not worry about a thing, that the FBI was on the case and had everything in hand. Then they walked out the front door and discovered that the cops had towed their car away.

Medlin was finally arrested but we never got back our 10,000 bucks, and we still don't know where Jimmy Hoffa is.

MORLEY SAFER:
Mickey Cohen is a former racketeer, an old friend of Jimmy Hoffa's, who was asked early on by the family to try and find out what happened.

COHEN:
Jimmy was done away with. He's buried in a lime pit.

SAFER:
Who did it?

COHEN:
I can't answer that . . . You see, I was away eleven years, you know. And it's a completely different ball game since I've come home. When Frank Costello was alive there was an absolute control. Nobody would get hit unless—unless it was a sit-down discussion or a roundtable discussion and then there was a decision brought down. But those days are long gone. Because if anybody in the world certainly didn't have—didn't deserve to have his lights put out, it was Jimmy Hoffa.

MIKE WALLACE:
What are the qualities that a hit man, a good hit man, should have?

DIAPOULAS:
. . . No conscience at all.

WALLACE:
And you have none?

DIAPOULAS:
Yeah, I have a conscience, sure. You know, there's limits to a hit. You hit a guy, you don't hit women, you don't hit children. You hit a guy that's in the mob, a guy that's an informer, a guy that's going to hurt the Family.

WALLACE:
Do you get paid? Is it piecework when you do a hit?

DIAPOULAS:
Well, when you do a hit you get prestige within the Family. You know, "You did a nice piece of work. *Bono salud.* Good man."

September 1976
February 1979

RATHER
SAFER
WALLACE

If you're a television producer and you're not a fan of Dan Rather's, then you should be in another business. So, when it became apparent in 1975 that we were going to need a third guy to help us carry the load, his was the only name in the hat. If Dan thought his career had come to a full stop after he traded barbs with Richard Nixon, he was the only one who did. He was just too good to go down for the count over a silly exchange like the one he and the President had had following a question the President didn't like during a televised news conference.

Nixon: Are you running for something?
Rather: No, sir, are you?

Those four little words had done it. Rather was now persona non grata with the Nixon crowd, but he hung in there until Nixon left office and then came to New York to front the *CBS Reports* series, but not for long.

Dan remembers his coming to *60 Minutes* this way:

"Let me get this straight," said Jean Rather. "Don Hewitt wants you to go to *60 Minutes?*"

"Yup," said I to my loyal helpmate, partner and wife.

"And what does Mike Wallace say? And Morley Safer. What's he say?"

"Dunno."

"Well, dammit, hoss—find out. If Mike and Morley want you, you'd be loco if you didn't take it; if they don't, you'd be loco if you did."

What Morley said was that he didn't really want a third correspondent on the broadcast, he didn't think one was needed, and he was worried about what an addition might do to the program's chemistry. But, he added, "If we're going to add somebody, I hope it's you."

Mike said, "Listen, my friend, we are going to have a third correspondent. We all want it to be you. There is no second choice."

Long pause.

Mike: "Well, whadda you say?"

Me: "Mike, I just don't know."

Mike: "Whadda you mean you don't know?"

Me: "I mean it sounds good and all that. But I'm just beginning to really feel good about *CBS Reports.*"

Mike: "Are you out of your mind? If you were a KGB agent looking for a place to hide, you couldn't find a better place than *CBS Reports.* Dan, Dan, Dan! Even Ed Murrow couldn't make *CBS Reports* fly. Come on. Don't be an idiot."

Me: "Mike, I'll think about it. Really think about it. And talk to Jean."

Mike: "Atta boy. Call me soon as she tells you to say yes."

I talked to Jean. We agreed there were risks. It was a gamble. "But," said she, "what the hell, we didn't come into this game checking."

Me: "Meaning what?"

Jean: "Tell 'em yes."

MORLEY SAFER:

**He came to Washington way back in 1933 as a messenger boy. By the time he left Congress in 1975, he had jurisdiction not only over the House floor, but the cloakroom, the rest-rooms, the barbershops—in short, the places where public men engage in private talk . . .
Fishbait, you say that 80 percent were hypocrites? . . . 80 percent pretty much were liars?**

FISHBAIT:

Yes, sir.

SAFER:

Eighty percent were serious sinners?

FISHBAIT:

Except on Sundays . . . There is always boozing and floozying . . . I don't have enough time to tell you everybody's name.

DAN RATHER:
The other great maestros are gone . . . But here is Stokowski, with his silver mane—old Stokie still at it, making beautiful music . . .

STOKOWSKI:
I always want to be first. I'm what is known as egocentric. It's a disease, a mental disease. I'm egocentric . . .

RATHER:
Is that part of what has kept your aspirations high?

STOKOWSKI:
No, it's because I've tried the opposite and it's boring.

JACKSON:
I look at a lot of these theories that a lot of the social workers come up with, and they say, now, the reason the Negro can't learn [is] his daddy's gone and his momma is pitiful and he doesn't understand anything about education and [there's] not much food in his refrigerator and there's rats all in the house and that's the reason he can't learn. And we read all that mess, and then we come to school . . . and the teacher stands there feeling guilty. Says, "These poor Negroes, they got all these heartaches and trials and tribulations and they're so pitiful and now I got to stand up here and try to teach them how to read and write and count." Well, if we can run faster and jump higher and shoot a basketball straight off of an inadequate diet, we can read and write and count off of those same diets.

JOHN LE CARRÉ
January 29, 1978

LE CARRÉ:

The taxi driver said, "What do you do for a living?" I said, "I'm a writer." He said, "What have you wrote?" I said *The Spy Who Came in from the Cold.* He said, "I know that." He said, "That had Richard Burton in it and the dog sniffed out the World Cup." . . . I said, "I'm terribly sorry. It's nothing of the sort. It had Richard Burton and—and Claire Bloom." And he said, "I took my wife to that and I'm beginning to think you're not who you say you are."

KFAF LASURIA
February 2, 1978

MORLEY SAFER:
Kfaf Lasuria, about to celebrate her one hundred and thirty-fifth birthday, [is] the oldest person in the Soviet Union, and possibly in the world. The year she was born . . . covered wagons were beginning to move out across the Humboldt Trail to California. And everyone remembered the Alamo; it happened only three years before she was born . . . Kfaf retired from her job as a farm worker just four years ago. She still takes a glass of vodka every morning, drinks wine with her meals and smokes two packs of cigarettes a day, plus a pipe or two of tobacco . . .

"HOW TO LIVE TO BE 100"

When you're in the news business, sometimes you get to go to exotic out-of-the-way places. Sometimes you get to go whether you want to or not because it's en route to someplace else. Abkhaz is not one of those places. First of all, it is not exotic, only out-of-the-way, and second of all, it's not en route to any place anyone would want to go. It's not that you can't get there from here. You can, but it's not easy. If you're going, it may be a good idea to stop in London and go to Harrod's and buy a pipe for Tarkun Lasuria's mother, who looks like Mammy Yokum.

Okay. Who is Tarkun Lasuria? Where is Abkhaz? Tarkun Lasuria is or was a ninety-four-year-old woodchopper. Today, if he's still alive, he's probably still chopping wood and if he's like his mother, he'll still be at it when he's a hundred and thirty-five. Abkhaz is a section of Georgia. No, not that Georgia! The one in Russia, where all those very old but very vigorous people live. Want a hint? Its biggest city is Sukhumi. Oh, that Abkhaz!

To get there, first you go to Moscow, then you take a long Aeroflot flight to Sukhumi on the shores of the Black Sea. There's only one hotel, and you'll do better getting a decent room if you go with Morley Safer, who knows every hotel room from Mombasa to Macon (in that other Georgia). Nothing ruffles Morley, unless it's a short Russian in his pajamas peering furtively out of a hotel room doorway, looking around to make sure no KGB agents are within earshot, and inquiring, "You Jewish?" Morley, looking around for KGB agents, snaps back, "Who wants to know?," and continues down the hall to his room, nervously awaiting the knock on the door that never comes.

So much for foreign intrigue. What were Morley and I and *60 Minutes* Producer John Tiffin doing in Abkhaz when we could have been in Marrakech or Macao? We were in Abkhaz because that's where the people are who live to be one hundred and over.

SAFER: Markhti Tarkil is a hundred and seven years old, yet he still works harder than many men in their fifties. It is difficult to verify these people's ages. Few documents exist. But Soviet and American researchers have devised a series of complicated tests designed to trap exaggeration and weed out false claims. Of 705 people tested, 95 percent were shown to have given their correct ages; and the remainder were within 5 percent of what they claimed. In some cases, there's evidence of being older than they claim . . .

Tarash Jopua is a hundred and three; his youngest daughter is twenty-two, born when he was eighty-one. A Georgian doctor told me it is not unusual for the sperm of a hundred -year-old man to still be active. His problem, he said, is finding a girl . . . For years it was believed that the secret of Abkhazian longevity was in their diet. Well, there's some truth, but their diet is no better or worse than that of country people in many places . . . Everything they eat is fresh. Their main source of carbohydrates is a kind of corn mush laboriously prepared for each meal. It's called "mamalika" and it tastes horrible to a non-Abkhazian palate. They also do not, as is commonly assumed, eat yogurt . . .

Despite their hospitality, they are small eaters. A study found they consume only about 1,800 calories a day, 600 less than is recommended by the U.S. Academy of Science for males over fifty-five. And their cholesterol level averages less than half the accepted normal amount for Americans between fifty and sixty years old. One almost constant factor among aged Abkhazians is that their parents, too, lived to their hundreds. So, all the mamalika in the world probably won't help you to a ripe old age if you have the wrong genes. Wine is taken at all meals, and Abkhazians call it "life-giving."

The morning after this story was on the air, we heard from Dannon, the yogurt people, who wanted to know, How do you get to Abkhaz? And once you get there, who do you see about making yogurt commercials? "They don't eat yogurt," Morley told them. "I said so on the program." They didn't want to hear that. All they wanted to know was how to get to Abkhaz? If Morley told them once, he told them ten times, "yogurt plays no part in their diet." No matter. It was going to play a part in Dannon's commercials.

ALBERTA HUNTER & EUBIE BLAKE
September 17, 1978

HUNTER:
I never got a chance to play the big time, you know? I had to always put on an Aunt Jemima dress, and so did Ethel Waters . . . They wouldn't let Negro women play the big time without doing that kind of thing. And then, if they did put us on a bill where there was [a] white singer, we'd always have to be second on the bill in order to warm it up.

BLAKE:
Your people, they knew better, but they didn't want to say that we had romances same as anybody else. So they never had a love song in a colored show. You couldn't stand up and sing, "Oh, darling, I love you."

TEDDY KOLLEK
September 24, 1978

MORLEY SAFER:
Jerusalem is a city—one in which taxes must be paid and parking tickets given and toilets flushed and dogs dissuaded from, as they say, fouling the footpath. On top of all those familiar urban delights, you have thirty-four Christian sects, plus Moslems and Jews, laying claim to various parts of Jerusalem or to the sum of its parts . . . And you have [Mayor] Teddy Kollek trying to keep the shrines and the body politic more or less intact. It's not easy.

KOLLEK:
There is no great difference whether I expropriate Jewish land or Arab land, with the exception of the hullabaloo in the world outside. But here, if you ask the people, the difference is simple. The Jews will call me a bastard and the Arabs will call me a Zionist bastard.

KANIN:

Of all the dangerous and destructive "isms" that have plagued this century, ageism is the most stupid . . . There's a story of a town in Connecticut that lost its power, had a complete outage. And they simply could not repair it [until] someone remembered that there was an old, old electrical engineer, who had installed the system in the first place, and he was living in some retirement community, and they sent for him. And he came along and he got a little mallet out and he went all through the [plant] and he went tap, tap, tap on a switch and all the lights came on. He sent the town a bill . . . for $1,000.02 . . . itemized as follows: Tapping, 2¢. Knowing where to tap, $1,000.

JEAN-PIERRE RAMPAL
October 15, 1978

MORLEY SAFER:
I don't think I've ever seen a great artist of any kind who is not good part ham.

RAMPAL:
Oh, yes, that's true, of course . . . You have to be a ham to go on the stage, and you have to be a ham to—to be excited because the people are applauding you . . . It starts waving over you . . . It's very important. [That's why] I hate to play in a church in someplace in Europe where the—the priest—priest? Priest?

SAFER:
Priest.

RAMPAL:
Priest, they don't applaud.

DAN RATHER:
Novelist Gore Vidal is an American who has lived and worked in Rome for the past twenty years.

VIDAL:
I can tell you one thing about fascism and Mussolini. The trains did not run on time. The trains were as late under Mussolini as they are today. Somebody once asked Mussolini, who apparently had a sense of humor, "Isn't it difficult, Duce, to govern the Italians?" He said, "It's not difficult. It's useless."

Murrieta
November 1, 1978

"THIS YEAR AT MURRIETA"

MIKE WALLACE: Each week *60 Minutes* gets more than a thousand letters, none more poignant than those describing miracle cures for cancer and other diseases. And lately we've gotten a surprising number about a particular cancer clinic on the grounds of a spa in Murrieta Hot Springs, California, where such "miracles" are supposedly being performed with lemon juice and distilled water . . .

We decided to make our own investigation. *60 Minutes* cameraman Greg Cook, *60 Minutes* soundman James Camery, and *60 Minutes* producer Marion Goldin, spent nine days at Murrieta to find out what it was really like. And because we'd been told the bottom line was dollars, we told them that soundman Camery, whom we dubbed "the Colonel," was a wealthy, semiretired investment counselor who had just learned he had leukemia; that cameraman Cook, a traveling photographer by trade, was his concerned nephew; that producer Goldin was the Colonel's longtime secretary. We rented a Rolls-Royce to impress them.

The *60 Minutes* team enrolled soundman Camery in the Murrieta cure program without revealing their identity, and they secretly filmed and recorded as much of the routine as possible. Camery paid $560 for the first week, although he was told he should plan on staying two weeks for a minimum of $1120. For that $560, he was examined once by the Murrieta doctor, Horace Gibson, who spends one day a week there. After looking in his eyes, Gibson assured Camery he did not have leukemia, but he didn't send him home, either. He discovered, instead, a leaky lung that he said was the source of Camery's difficulties. During the days that followed, what little monitoring of Camery there was was done by so-called "counselors" or "testers," none of them doctors. One of them told us he used to sell floor coverings; another was an embalmer's assistant . . . They tried to explain the unique way they could measure Camery's progress—through urine and saliva tests. Twice a day, they would test his urine, coming up with a mysterious set of numbers that, fed through a computer, supposedly reflected the state of his improving health . . . We pretended to keep soundman Camery on the routine. He pretended to drink only distilled water and lemon juice, but in fact he was eating a good deal more than that. We brought him breakfast and lunch in his room, and supervision was so lax we had no trouble taking him out for dinner. And just to see if they could tell if there were special problems apparent in Camery's urine,

on two occasions we substituted cameraman Cook's urine for soundman Camery's; on another, we gave them producer Goldin's. Nonetheless, we were told by Camery's counselor that his urine number showed he was making remarkable progress, especially during his fast . . .

R. J. Rudd is the promoter of the Murrieta Health Clinic. Calling himself a Baptist minister, Rudd preaches every Sunday at the Murrieta Chapel . . . Unaware that he was being filmed and recorded, it didn't take him long before he pressed us to invest, tantalizing us with prospects not of curing ills, but of a remarkable tax shelter . . .

By this time, my associates had learned enough about the questionable medical practices, about big money deals, indeed about promoter Rudd's own background, that they decided it was time for me to get involved. So I arrived the following Sunday morning with another film crew, and began to ask R. J. Rudd some straight questions. At this point he had no idea of my relationship with Goldin, Cook and Camery . . .

WALLACE: You're not a medical doctor?

RUDD: No, I'm not.

WALLACE: You're an economist?

RUDD: I'm a . . . I have a Ph.D.

WALLACE: In?

RUDD: In economics and one in philosophy. And I also am a full-time licensed ordained minister of the Gospel. My two Ph.D.'s, one came from the Tennessee University.

WALLACE: University of Tennessee?

RUDD: No, the Christian Tennessee University. And I got one from Florida—Tennessee—Let's see. Trinity Christian College in Florida . . .

WALLACE: Where is that?

RUDD: It's in—I believe that now they're presently in Fort Lauderdale.

WALLACE: Well, [the diploma] says here it was signed and sealed at Brownsville, Texas.

RUDD: Okay, that was a branch of that operation, you see.

WALLACE: And this is the [diploma from] Tennessee Christian University. And where is this university? What town?

RUDD: It's—I believe that one is close to—let me think of the name just a minute. Chattanooga.

WALLACE: Education officials in all three states subsequently told us those diplomas were nothing more than mail-order degrees from nonexistent universities. As for religion, Baptist Church officials have had to deny many times that he was ever ordained a Baptist minister.

I also asked Rudd about the mysterious computer to decipher those urine and saliva numbers that he kept talking about.

Where's the master computer?

RUDD: It'll be probably somewhere in California here.

WALLACE: You don't have it set up yet?

RUDD: Oh, yes, we do.

WALLACE: Where?

RUDD: In the Los Angeles area.

WALLACE: Well, can we take a look at it?

RUDD: No. We can't let—let that out yet.

WALLACE: Many . . . would say there's a kind of a con-game operation going on at Murrieta Springs . . .

RUDD: This is not a con game. I feel it's a sincere effort by a lot of good people who are giving some of the best years of their life here to—to build a retreat program where people can come and get nutritional assistance.

Shortly after we drove out of Murietta, the State of California drove in. Before they got through with R. J. Rudd, they put him away for seven years for conspiracy and fraud. But between the time he was indicted and the time he landed in the slammer, he fled to Costa Rica, where he peddled gold-mining certificates to retired Americans. When the retirees caught on to the fact that what they were buying was worthless, Rudd offered to trade them bonds for the certificates. The bonds, however, were from the Weimar Republic, which was put out of business by Hitler in the 1930s. Shortly after he got to Lompoc Prison in California, he began organizing his fellow convicts into a movement to go to Costa Rica to serve their parole time—a million dollars plus a free home if they relocate there under his new program. I wouldn't be a bit surprised if someday R. J. Rudd and *60 Minutes* meet up again.

WHY WOULD SOMEONE WHO IS OBVIOUSLY A CROOK GO ON *60 MINUTES?* AND OTHER QUESTIONS I'M OFTEN ASKED

Once, Morley Safer and I went to Philadelphia to pick up the Liberty Bell award, which really impressed me when I found out that the first recipient was Milton Berle. Now, I felt, we had really made it.

During a question and answer session following the awards lunch, someone asked Morley why a guy who was obviously a crook would agree to go on *60 Minutes*. Morley's answer was a gem: "A crook doesn't believe he's made it as a crook until he's been on *60 Minutes*."

The real answer is, I guess, that most of the so-called "crooks" you've met on *60 Minutes* were con men like R. J. Rudd of the Murrieta cancer-cure program. Or Harold Goldstein, who sold phony stock options. Or Ernest Sinclair, who would sell you a college degree from the college of your choice for up to $3,000. These guys, and anyone else who has been conning the public and getting away with it, can't believe they can't also get away with conning *60 Minutes*.

Before *60 Minutes* I had never heard the term "ambush journalism" or "confrontation journalism." The terms were invented, as far as I know, by newspaper people who thought we were being unfair to some of the people we caught red-handed on *60 Minutes*. As I told the *60 Minutes* staff at the end of the 1983–1984 television season, "Confrontation is not a dirty word . . . Sometimes it's the best kind of journalism as long as you don't confront people just for the sake of a confrontation," and I don't believe we ever do, but because other television organizations thought "confrontation" or "ambush" was the way to build ratings they jumped in with both feet—both left feet. Because they did it so badly we got the fallout. No one has ever been confronted by *60 Minutes* without our first trying to arrange a meeting and without our first knowing that he or she was involved in some sort of misdeed. It may sometimes look to a viewer as if we have taken someone by surprise, but believe me, that's not the case. The scamps and rascals know damned well why we're there. As my wife says (and she should know—after she was the Washington *Post*'s diplomatic correspondent, she was NBC's White House correspondent): "To make an omelette you

have to break eggs. When newspaper reporters do it, no one sees them, but when TV reporters do it everybody watches!"

My favorite question from television columnists is: Aren't you guys really more show biz than news biz? First of all, in the sense that we do not deal with the news of the last twenty-four hours or even the news of the last week, we are not, strictly speaking, news biz. We are, for want of a better word, "reality" biz, as opposed to make-believe biz. What concerns us are the times in which we live; whether that is "news" depends on your definition of "news." Mine has always been that "news" is anything that has happened, is happening or will happen in the times in which we live that people are interested in hearing about for the first time or in hearing more about. As for the show biz aspects of the broadcast, show me a good newspaper that doesn't have some show biz in its soul. What do you think a headline is but a barker beckoning you into the tent? I'm always amused when one of those holier-than-thou television columnists who claims *60 Minutes* is more "entertainment" than "news" issues a sermon about it from a pulpit that sits smack-dab in the middle of gossip columns, advice to the lovelorn columns, horoscopes and word games, cheek by jowl with Garfield the Cat and Beatle Bailey. Sure, there is a line that separates news biz from show biz. The trick is to walk up to it, touch it with your toe but not cross it. If you cross that line, you lose your credibility. (Oops, I wanted to write a book without once using the word "credibility.")

Another question is: Why are you guys opposed to big business? We're not. We are, ourselves, big business. At the height of the season, commercials on *60 Minutes* sometimes go for better than $350,000 a minute, and we've got six and a half of those minutes to sell every Sunday night. So far be it from us to look askance at big business. On the other hand, I think big business sometimes tends to look askance at us, as it sometimes tends to look askance at journalism in general. A business, big, medium or small, wants only two things said about it: What it pays its public relations people to say and what it pays its advertising agency to say. Can't blame them for that. If I were an electronics company, I'd love to go through life with the public's only conception of me being "The quality goes in before the name goes on," or if I were a cigarette company, I'd love it if the whole world thought my middle name was "low tar and low nicotine"; if I were a car company, I'd be pleased as punch if people thought everyone who worked for me was named "Mr. Goodwrench." When someone starts looking around, behind or under those slogans, the people who pay for them get very upset. I would, too, but I'm not too sure that taking a good hard look from time to time at how the free enterprise system works is necessarily a bad thing for the free enterprise system.

ARTHUR FIEDLER
November 26, 1978

MORLEY SAFER:
Pops—there are really two of them: the orchestra [called] the Boston Pops; and "Pops" himself, Arthur Fiedler, who's been conducting that orchestra for almost fifty years . . . If you believe what you read about Arthur Fiedler, people will tell you that he's curmudgeonly, mean, a skinflint, has got a terrible temper. Can that be true?

FIEDLER:
I think all those things are more or less true, yes . . .

SAFER:
[But] you would think that a man who gets [as much adulation as you get] would be in love with people.

FIEDLER:
Well, I think a great number of people are bores, really, and the adulation—just words.

DAN RATHER:
Human rights is one of the cornerstones of President Carter's foreign policy. But do our friends get off easier than our enemies when it comes to respecting the rights of their people? Case in point: Somoza of Nicaragua . . .
General, I've been told your wealth is in the neighborhood of $500 million . . .

SOMOZA:
I think we're around $100 million . . .

RATHER:
General, what goes through your mind, how do you address your conscience when you see the faces of all these poor people in Nicaragua . . . ?

SOMOZA:
I wish I had more wealth so they could be wealthier.

KATHARINE HEPBURN
January 14, 1979

HEPBURN:
. . . We must reform, and I don't know how we're going to reform. We're sitting looking at a lot of filth. And I'm disgusted with the movies, disgusted, because they're kidding themselves into saying it's a sort of intellectual pastime. Bunk! It's 42nd Street filth being sold for too much . . . And the critics, I think, have lost their minds . . .

MORLEY SAFER:
I know you're not advocating censorship, but—

HEPBURN:
Oh, don't be too sure.

"HEPBURN"

From the day we went on the air I had wanted to get Katharine Hepburn on *60 Minutes,* and when Jim Jackson, a *60 Minutes* producer, came to me and said he had a fighting chance of getting her to sit down with Morley Safer, I was delighted. A "fighting chance" was a lot farther than we had gotten before.

Jim had had some conversations with Warner Brothers, for whom she was making the television movie of *The Corn Is Green.* They were shooting it just outside London, and the producer of the movie said he'd pave the way for us to get her on *60 Minutes.* So off Jim went to London.

"Miss Hepburn," the producer said, "this is Jim Jackson from *60 Minutes.*"

"Yes?" she said politely but very coolly. She was in make-up and costume as Miss Moffat, the Welsh schoolteacher, and it was clear that she considered doing a television interview an intrusion she had no intention of putting up with.

It's "foolish" she told Jim in her dressing room, where she literally, but not figuratively, let down her hair, which had been pinned up for the role. During the next ten minutes, as she worked on her hair, she gave Jim ten good reasons why she would never go on a television show. He countered with ten good reasons why she should.

The brush strokes got faster and faster as she warmed to her subject. "I'd be a damned fool to go on . . . I have absolutely nothing to say . . . I'll just be repeating myself . . . People will think I'm a total bore . . ."

But she did agree to meet Morley Safer in London when he arrived and agreed to let Jim sort of hang around the studio during the filming of *The Corn Is Green.* So Jim began to spend his days at the studio, and at first she very pointedly ignored him. It was George Cukor, her director, who finally broke the ice. He kidded her unmercifully and asked Jim in front of her, "Why are you doing her? She can't even remember her lines. Do a profile of me. I'm much more interesting than she is."

"Listen to the old fool," she said. "I'm doing most of the directing myself."

But since Cukor had befriended Jim, and since she spent most of her time between takes with Cukor, she had no choice but to begin chatting with Jim. When Safer arrived, he and Hepburn eyed each other politely, but she still wouldn't agree to an interview. "Certainly not in London while I'm working," she said. Jim then asked her, "Just in case we eventually do the interview, could we make some shots of you working?" She seemed wary but she said it would be all right.

The next day a film crew from our London bureau arrived. The minute she spotted them she panicked. "It's impossible. I cannot do my lines in front of one camera and turn around and be staring into another camera. I won't have a chance to breathe. I know I told you yesterday that it would be all right. But I am in an absolute panic today at the mere thought of it. Look, I know this has been expensive for a crew to come here. Tell me how much it comes to. I'll write you a check this instant for the whole amount. Just get them out of here."

We backed off fast, but asked if we could just take wide shots of the set from the catwalks above the studio. She said okay. As we began taking our wide shots, some of the movie crew began helping on the sly, opening up scenery to give us a better view. Jan Morgan, our cameraman, then decided to move off the catwalk onto the floor. Hepburn was aware that we were no longer shooting from overhead, but by then she had relaxed and was actually enjoying our sneaking around.

That afternoon her producer told Jim that if he needed a lift back to London, Miss Hepburn had offered to drop him off at his hotel after work. She had gotten to like Jim, and during the ride they talked like two old friends. She talked about her early days in Hollywood and told stories about the making of *The Philadelphia Story.* Jim asked her about Spencer Tracy. Would she talk about him? She said she would never talk about Spencer Tracy—about her private life with him—as long as Mrs. Tracy was still alive. But she would talk about working with him. She went on and on. What she was giving Jim, he realized later, was a layout for an interview. She had obviously prepared for the car ride, letting Jim know her strengths, what topics she was good at, what interested her and what bored her. Jim remembers thinking: Oh my God. I'm in a limousine in London with Katharine Hepburn. Somebody take my picture.

The next time he heard from her was when he got a call in NewYork letting him know that she had agreed to do the interview in Manhattan, and when Jim and Morley arrived at her house she greeted them like old friends. She took them on a tour of the house and after the interview insisted on making lunch for the camera crew. She even rode a bike in the New York traffic so we could match a shot of her riding a bike in *The Corn Is Green.* Jim was satisfied after the first take, but she insisted on doing it again and again, weaving through the traffic, because, she said, "There wasn't enough conflict for me." Finally, when she was almost sideswiped by a truck, she was satisfied.

Were we satisfied?

Were we ever.

SAFER: I don't believe in lists, but every time somebody compiles a list of the most admired women, there's Katharine Hepburn.

HEPBURN: Yes, but this becomes the style. It doesn't mean much, does it?

SAFER: No, but there's got to be something there.

HEPBURN: Well, all my contemporaries have died off, so I'm the only one that's left. I'm in a safe group. I haven't got the romantic feeling about age. I think we rot away, and it's too goddamn bad we do . . . A friend of mine called and she said . . . "I called a friend of mine and said, 'How do you feel?' And there was a long pause, and the woman said, 'Well, I feel fine, if you don't ask for details.'" I mean that's an absolutely divine remark . . .

SAFER: How do you account for the success of the Tracy-Hepburn pictures? What was the chemistry on that screen?

HEPBURN: I think we were the perfect American male and female.

SAFER: An idealized version of the American couple?

HEPBURN: Not so idealized. I mean, she was a scrapper and tried to boss him around, and he just pushed her off at the right moment . . . Well now, mind you—mind you, I don't think it's any great art, because you have to just—Spencer always used to say, "Remember who killed Lincoln." And I said look at Shirley Temple. You know, she was three and she was great. She could laugh and cry and carry on.

SAFER: At any point when you were young, wanting to be an actor, did you have doubts at all? Say, "Well, if it doesn't work out, I'll try something else"?

HEPBURN: Oh, yes. Oh, yes. But I was driven by love. You're driven by love . . . I came to this city, I was so shy that I never went to a restaurant. I won't go to a restaurant now.

SAFER: But you're not that shy anymore.

HEPBURN: In a different way.

SAFER: You don't go out to restaurants?

HEPBURN: I don't go to restaurants because they charge $60 a meal, and I can serve you here anytime you want to come. You give me the $60, and I'll give you dinner.

SAFER: Are you a bit of a—how should I say this—

HEPBURN: Tight.

SAFER: —tight?

HEPBURN: No, I'm not tight. I just don't like injustice . . . I carry a hard-boiled egg and a piece of ham, and I take hot water out of the tap and put it on coffee, sugar, and carry fruit of some sort, and a breakfast tray, and it costs me five cents . . .

SAFER: You've led such an extraordinarily independent life, and you do it yourself, whether it's fixing the car or reglazing a window. If you hadn't been an actress, what would have been?

HEPBURN: I never thought. I would have tormented some man, I suppose, and had about eight children. And tormented them!

DAN RATHER:
If you thought you had seen and heard everything you needed to know about Watergate, so did we—until Judge John Sirica, who presided over the Watergate trial, decided to tell his story [to CBS News correspondent Fred Graham]. . .

FRED GRAHAM:
What would [you] have done if Nixon had refused [to turn over the tapes]?

SIRICA:
[Nixon] had a beautiful home down there in Miami, a beautiful home out in San Clemente. He loved money . . . And I said if I hit him in his pocketbook, he'll come around fast. So, I decided to fine him . . . I had a figure of between $25,000 and $50,000 for every day he refused to turn those tapes over. I didn't think he'd last more than a day or two.

REASONER
RATHER
SAFER
WALLACE

Harry Reasoner was there at the beginning and it was Harry who set the tone on our very first broadcast. (Remember, we were a new breed of cat. Nothing exactly like us had ever been seen on television before.) On September 24, 1968, he put it this way: "The symphony of the real world is not a monotone and while this does not mean you have to mix it all up in one broadcast, it seems to us that the idea of a flexible attitude has its attractions. All art is the rearrangement of previous perceptions and we don't claim this is anything more than that or even that journalism is an art but we do think this is a sort of new approach."

That "sort of new approach" spawned so many imitations that by now most of us have forgotten the names of all but one or two of them. What they lacked was style and that's something you can never have too much of. Even though we already had television's two heaviest hitters in Mike and Dan, what I wanted in 1979 was another stylish pitcher like Morley who could thread a needle with a well-turned phrase. One of the first stories Harry did after coming back from ABC was the kind of story he and we do best—one of those "I didn't know *that*" stories. It was called "The Keepin' of the Green."

REASONER: For all the centuries since the Celts first came to this green and poor land, Ireland's most dependable product has been the people who could use its language—the minstrel Gaelic and then the particular Irish-English, lilting, perceptive and poignant. But for those same centuries the anomaly has been that the land drove these singers out to do their work elsewhere—James Joyce, Bernard Shaw, all the people who brightened other places with what they brought from here. Now a modern law is trying to change all that. It says if you make money from making creations—books, paintings, sculptures, symphonies—you can keep it, all of it. No income tax. It is admittedly a discriminatory law, which would certainly be challenged in the United States, but Ireland doesn't have a constitution like ours. What Ireland has is a conscience—a guilty one. J.P. Donleavy, now an Irish citizen, may be the foremost paradox of that law. He came here as a student on the G.I. Bill after World War II. His books tend to be critical of the Irish and the Irish have banned them on moral gounds. But their profits elsewhere flow back to him untaxed and provide him with a 400-acre estate, a Georgian manor with 25 rooms and an indoor swimming pool.

DONLEAVY: In some way one feels it's almost a justice, in terms of the things that, say, James Joyce must have gone through. It's a redressing of previous wrong.

REASONER: So it's a good thing for literature.

DONLEAVY: Oh, yes. I regard it as important, if not more important, than the Nobel Prize.

See what I mean? You didn't know that, did you?

JOHNNY CARSON
September 23, 1979

MIKE WALLACE:
Are you reluctant, in [doing] your monologue, to go hard on a guy?

CARSON:
When [Congressman] Wilbur Mills had his problem . . . I stopped doing jokes [about him] as soon as people found out he was an alcoholic . . .

WALLACE:
Of course, it takes one to know one.

CARSON:
Aah! Cruel. You're cruel.

WALLACE:
[Ed McMahon] told us that from time to time you were going to take on the whole Russian army, and he—and you didn't have the bazookas to do it.

CARSON:
That's right. That's one reason I found that it's probably best for me not to tangle with it.

MIKE WALLACE:
Governor, did you really say more people died at Chappaquidick . . . than at Three Mile Island?

CONNALLY:
No, I did not.

WALLACE;
You're sure?

CONNALLY:
I'm positive.

WALLACE:
If I could show it to you on tape?

CONNALLY:
If you [could]—you were taping something you shouldn't have been taping.

VOLODYA POSNER
January 6, 1980

HARRY REASONER:

We talked about journalism to Volodya Posner, a [Moscow television] commentator whose parents were Soviet officials living in New York when he grew up, accounting for his completely American English . . .
In programming in general, what's the emphasis on? Is it on cultural [events] . . . or on education or propaganda?

POSNER:

Well, propaganda's an ambiguous word. I believe Woody Guthrie used to say that to the five-year-old little boy who doesn't want to go to sleep a lullaby is propaganda.

MIKE WALLACE:
It's a new year—everyplace, that is, except at Boston University. There, it seems, the more things change, the more they are the same, because for years BU's "BMOC"—Bad Man on Campus—has had that place in an uproar. The BMOC is John Silber, president of Boston University.

SILBER:
A university is certainly not a democracy, if it is any good. The more democratic a university becomes the lousier it becomes . . . When I first came here I was asked by the students to visit the dormitories, and I was supposed to discover how bad they were architecturally. What I discovered was that most of the rooms were filthy. And I came out with the conclusion that, evidently, the students believed that filth was a cultural achievement.

BETTE DAVIS
January 20, 1980

DAVIS:
"I'd love to kiss you but I just washed my hair." . . . [That's] my favorite line in any movie I ever did. [Michael] Curtiz was so against my playing this kind of a part, because, he said, "That's the unsexiest looking woman I have ever seen in my life." . . . And [Richard] Barthelmess wouldn't even test with me, so I had to end up kissing the lens . . . Every scene I played, [Curtiz] would say, "Goddamn lousy actress."

LEONARD BERNSTEIN
February 10, 1980

MIKE WALLACE:
Serge Koussevitzky, the man who led the Boston Symphony years ago, . . . was Bernstein's idol, and Kousse adored the young Lenny, nurtured him, saw his infinite possibilities. But Koussevitzky worried that one thing would stand in Bernstein's way.

BERNSTEIN:
It is the name, the *nom*. He said, "It will be open for you all the gates from the world, but it will nothing happen [if] you will not change it the *nom*." And then he proposed the *nom* that I should change it to, which was "Leonard S. Berns." I lost a night's sleep over it and came back and told him I had decided to make it as Leonard Bernstein, or not at all.

HARRY REASONER:
An elder statesman, by one definition, is a leader in whom the fires of personal ambition have been banked. From the coals, the nation then gets wisdom and candor. Well, Barry Goldwater is sort of our elder statesman . . . even to some of the Americans who voted against him in 1964 . . . Did [Richard Nixon] hurt conservatism and the Republicans?

GOLDWATER:
Mr. Nixon hurt the Republican Party and he hurt America and, frankly, I don't think he should ever be forgiven. He came as close to destroying this country as any one man in that office ever has come.

MORLEY SAFER:
Just three months after Pearl Harbor [Charles Lindbergh] made a speech saying the British, FDR and the Jews were trying to get us into a war.

LINDBERGH:
I was horrified . . . I said, "I think it's worse to rouse anti-Semitism in the country, much worse than war." He was not a great reader. Had he read Goebbels and Hitler, he would have known that people who are really anti-Semitic start with these statements.

SAFER:
Did you love him less for that?

LINDBERGH:
I can't say I did, but I pitied him.

RIEFENSTAHL:
Look here what is written . . . that I danced naked for Hitler . . .

DAN RATHER:
It's a lie?

RIEFENSTAHL:
It's a lie.

RATHER:
You were not Hitler's pinup?

RIEFENSTAHL:
No, not a little bit.

RATHER:
Or his mistress?

RIEFENSTAHL:
Not a bit. Not one day, not one minute.

"ONE OF HITLER'S FAVORITES"

Leni Riefenstahl was no ordinary eighty-year-old. She was an eighty-year-old former actress turned film maker who in the 1930s had made for Adolf Hitler two of his favorite propaganda films. She was doing underwater photography off the reefs of the little Bahamian island of San Salvador when she agreed to an interview with *60 Minutes.*

At her first meeting with Jeanne Solomon, our producer on the story, she had said she wouldn't answer any questions about her relations with Hitler or even about her role in the Nazi propaganda machine, but once the interview began she kept bringing up subjects she had told Dan Rather and Jeanne were verboten. However, when Dan asked her a question about the Nazi era, she burst into tears, got up and locked herself in the toilet. Boy, was she smart. She knew from her own experience with a camera when the film was about to run out, so she saved her outbursts for those last seconds before we had to stop and change rolls.

Dan was nonplussed. From conversations they had had before the interview started he was sure that whatever Hitler felt for Leni Riefenstahl—love or just plain admiration—there was no love lost between her and Josef Goebbels, Hitler's propaganda minister. He gave her a hard time about her films and didn't seem to give two pfennigs that she was a buddy of Hitler's. *That* drove her up the wall. No matter whether she wanted to answer them or not, it was our job at least to raise the questions.

When Jeanne finally talked her out of the toilet they resumed the interview. Dan was his usual calm, cool, collected self as he sat there trying to catch the crazy signals she was giving off. One minute it was okay to talk about Hitler and the Nazis; the next it wasn't.

The mail that came in after the story ran was mixed. Some viewers criticized Dan for beating up on an old lady. Others said we had let her off the hook and treated her too nicely because she was an old lady. Riefenstahl herself wrote to Jeanne to say that she didn't blame her or Dan for asking her about Hitler. She said she knew they were only following orders.

Sound familiar?

DAN RATHER:
Mr. President, you recently directed your staff to make report cards on their employees. Now, in specific areas I'm going to ask you to grade yourself A though F. Foreign policy?

CARTER:
You put me on the spot. I would say maybe a B or a C-plus . . . Let's say B-minus.

RATHER:
Overall domestic policy?

CARTER:
Under the circumstances, I think about a B . . . maybe a C.

RATHER:
And on leadership?

CARTER:
. . . Maybe a B.

TRICKS OF THE TRADE

One night when I was doing the Cronkite News, a plane crashed in New York's East River taking off from La Guardia. It happened during a tug-boat strike, and nothing was moving on the river except for a tug from New Haven whose crew was outside the jurisdiction of the unions involved in the strike. By the time I got to where the tug was bringing in bodies, the other networks, as well as all the independents and the wire services and newspapers, were setting up to interview the tugboat captain about what he had seen out there at the crash site.

We all packed into the wheelhouse and the captain began telling his story. About the time he got to the goriest part, with all the newsmen hanging on his every word, I interrupted his account of the "burning bodies" and "groaning survivors" with what struck the rest of the crowd as a completely irrelevant question.

"Who owns this tug?"

"For Christ sake, Hewitt," the news guys said. "Who cares?"

"New Haven Tug," the captain said.

"Okay, Hewitt," the boys said. "No more dumb questions. Captain, please start again."

As he started again, about the "burning bodies" and the "groaning survivors," I sneaked out of the wheelhouse and went to a phone booth on the dock.

"Call New Haven Tug," I told the editor on duty back in the CBS newsroom, "and tell them we want to charter their boat."

When I got back to the wheelhouse the captain was still going strong and they all gave me the "shush" sign and whispered not to interrupt again with meaningless questions.

Meaningless to you guys, I thought, not to me.

Before the captain had finished, the phone rang in the wheelhouse and he stopped to answer it.

"Which one of you guys is Hewitt?" the captain asked.

"I am."

"Okay, the boat is under charter to you. What do you want to do?"

"First thing I want to do is get these guys off my boat."

You could get killed doing things like that, but the tug crew was put to work clearing the decks of everyone except the CBS camera crew. They even found one or two stowaways before we sailed off at first light for the scene of the wreck, with an angry mob on the dock shaking their fists at us.

The captain, incidentally, thought it was great fun. About an hour later an NBC crew came out in a rowboat with an outboard motor and a small transmitter with which they hoped to get pictures back to the *Today* show.

I looked over the side at their little boat and then I got a nasty idea. "If we maneuver between them and the Empire State Building," I told the captain, "they won't be able to get a signal back to NBC."

As I said, the captain was having fun and he thought that was a dandy idea. But during the maneuver he rammed them accidentally. No harm was done but they were pretty damned mad.

When I got back, my boss said, "What the hell is the matter with you?"

"What do you mean—what's the matter with me?"

"We got a call from NBC that you tried to sink their boat in the East River."

"Cry babies," I said.

Will the Convention Please Come to Order!

Nowhere is the competition between the networks more ridiculous than at political conventions. The year 1956 was the year we tried to get the jump on the other networks by running a school for convention delegates to tell them how to act on television. Boy, was that a mistake! What we told them, mostly, was not to pick their noses or scratch their crotches because you never know when the camera is watching. It was better when they picked their noses and scratched their crotches, and it was better when it was *their* convention and not *ours*.

By 1960, however, the conventions had become as much ours as theirs. I mean, a network is not going to show up six hundred strong in a strange city just to let the politicians show off. We come to town like Ringling Brothers, even though most of the feudin', the fussin' and the fightin' is over before the convention even begins. That leaves us little to do but show off our finery and trot out our best performers and make sure what's going on in NBC's ring or ABC's ring is less exciting than what's going on in ours.

The first thing we do when we get to town is hoist a sign over our anchor booth. So do NBC and ABC. Those signs are so big and dominate the hall so much that everything else—even the podium we've come to cover—pales by comparison. When I first started covering political conventions you used to see a good credentials fight once in a while or a good platform fight, even though the battlers usually kissed and made up before they went home. Today, if you want to see a good fight at a political convention, let one network's sign be a micrometer larger than the next guy's.

All three networks are so good at what they do, especially their evening newscasts, which are superb, that I am mystified as to why we allow ourselves to go off the deep end every four years for an event of marginal significance. But we do, and never was that more apparent than in the summer of 1964 at the Republican Convention in San Francisco that nominated Barry Goldwater.

In the CBS contingent were Bob Wussler (who always seemed to be there when the devil got the better of me) and Bill Leonard, who was in charge of our political coverage. In the row in front of us at a preliminary meeting with the Republican National Committee was the NBC contingent. At one point I glanced down and noticed that the NBC man in front of me had accidentally kicked back under his seat a book titled *NBC Convention Plans*, which was practically resting on my shoe. I gulped. In that book had to be gold. I poked Leonard and gestured toward the floor. He gulped and whispered, "Take it." Pretending to tie my shoe, I bent down and stole it. Now the trick was to get it out of the room without attracting any attention. That turned out to be so easy that I got overconfident. Instead of taking it to a library to read or mailing it to myself in New York like any felon worth his salt would have done, I took it back to my room at the Fairmont. A few minutes later Wussler arrived. While the two of us were poring over it, trying to make head or tail of what NBC was up to, there was a knock on the door.

It was Scotty Connal, a former hockey player who was now a unit manager for NBC. Although I never found out for sure, I always suspected that Elmer Lower, then President of ABC News, had seen me take the book and had ratted on me because a brouhaha between NBC and CBS could only be good for ABC. Anyway, there was Scotty at the door. "Where's my book?" he demanded.

"What book?" I asked.

"You know what book," Scotty replied.

"Okay," I said to Wussler, "we've been caught so let's give him his book"—as if we had a choice. Remember, Scotty had played hockey and he was big. Ready for the punch in the mouth that never came, I heaved a sigh of relief when Scotty said, "Thank you. You don't know how scared I was. If I hadn't found it, I probably would have been fired." (Letting an NBC book fall into CBS hands was like letting the D-Day plans fall into the hands of the German High Command. You could get shot.) He added that he had been so desperate to get it he would have thrown me out the window if I hadn't handed it over. We all laughed at that, shook hands, parted friends, and I dismissed the incident as no more than a shenanigan gone awry. The next morning I had forgotten all about it. Then I opened my hotel room door and picked up the San Francisco *Chronicle*. There, on page one, was an eight-column banner headline shouting: THE BATTLE OF THE TV EXECUTIVES. "Hot damn," I thought, "Aubrey's in trouble again." Jim Aubrey was the top man at CBS Television and had the same low opinion of news people that we had of him. This, I thought, was going to be good. It was, but it wasn't about Aubrey. It was about me. And it began: "An NBC unit manager yesterday threatened to throw a CBS director out of the tenth floor window of the Fairmont Hotel."

Crazy things happened at conventions. In 1952, before anyone had come up with an electronic means of superimposing names over pictures on the screen instantaneously, it was a long laborious process to set up a name in type and have it photostatted so it could be superimposed on the screen. White letters on a black background work best. We did it so the audience could tell who was who without our having to interrupt the speeches. It wasn't till much later that we learned that interrupting political speeches wasn't necessarily a bad thing. Anyway, the problem of how to set up the type in a hurry seemed to have no easy solution, and I was pondering it one morning as I sat in a diner not far from Lake Shore Drive.

"What'll you have?" the waitress said.

"I'll have that board," I answered.

"What board?" she said, looking at me like I was one of those crazies you sometimes sit next to in diners.

"What do you call that thing up there on the wall," I said, "the one with today's menu and the prices."

"I don't know what you call it," she said. "What'll you have?" By now I was convinced that, no matter what, I had to have that board. If you could spell out "French Fries" and "Pork Chops" with those little white letters, you could also spell out Estes Kefauver and Everett Dirksen. So I struck a deal with the owner. For twenty-five bucks with my orange juice, toast and coffee thrown in, he took it off the wall and handed it to me along with a box of little white letters.

What happened right after the Republicans chose Richard Nixon to be Ike's running mate was also "off the wall," though maybe not so literally as that menu board. Nixon was holding an impromptu news conference in a hallway leading from the convention floor, where he had just been raised to the pinnacle of a vice-presidential candidate. NBC, ABC and CBS were carrying the news conference live on radio and television. As usual, it was a mob scene. Our man in the crowd was Bill Downs, who was wearing a headset on which he could hear Walter Cronkite and Ed Murrow in the anchor booth and me when I wanted to cut in and tell him something. He was also holding the microphone over which we were picking up what Nixon was saying. All of a sudden I was struck with a crazy thought. "Take off your headset, Bill," I said, "and put it on Nixon before he has a chance to know what's happening, and tell him Cronkite and Murrow want to talk to him."

Downs couldn't answer because his mike was "hot" and Nixon was speaking into it, as he was speaking into a dozen or so other mikes that were stuck in his face. Bill thought I had lost my mind, but he did what I told him. He took off his headset and stuck it on Nixon's head, handed him his mike and told him, "Walter Cronkite and Ed Murrow want to talk to you."

Because it happened so fast and because it happened live in front of millions, Nixon had no chance to think about it. The other reporters didn't know what to do because there was nothing they *could* do. Here was Richard Nixon, wearing a CBS headset and holding a CBS microphone, talking to Murrow and Cronkite live on NBC and ABC as well as on CBS. We, of course, could carry both ends of the conversation. What the others got were only long pauses and then his answers, which began, "Well, Ed" or "Well, Walter." It was delicious.

Putting a headset on news personalities at news events so they could talk to Cronkite became a CBS trademark. It didn't make the reporters on the scene, even the CBS reporters, very happy though. Hughes Rudd, when he worked for us, once said he'd had a dream that I told him to take off his headset and put it on Cronkite so Walter could have a conversation with himself.

Husking Corn in Iowa

When Harry Reasoner, Charles Kuralt and I went to Iowa to cover Nikita Khrushchev's visit to a farm owned by a man named Garst, we had with us Bobby Wussler, soon to become Robert Wussler, later to become our president. But it's a miracle that both our careers, his and mine, didn't end right there in a cornfield in Iowa. After staying up most of the night going over how we were going to deploy our cameras to cover the Russian Premier's visit, we went out to the Garst farm about six the next morning to see if we had overlooked anything. (What we didn't do was "finalize" our "game plan" because in 1959 no one talked that way.) It was barely dawn when we came across the NBC remote truck parked on a dirt road near the farm. A remote truck is a giant van that houses a complete control room and everything else needed to put on a broadcast. Mostly they're used for sports events. I don't know why, but that remote truck with its big NBC lettering on the side looked particularly inviting sitting there all alone in the early morning sun. What made it more inviting were the keys in the ignition.

Without saying a word, I looked at Wussler. I didn't have to say anything; he knew what I was thinking.

"You wouldn't dare," he said.

"Try me," I said.

"You don't have the guts."

"I have the guts," I told him, "but what in hell would we do with it?"

"Hide it in a cornfield," Wussler said. "They won't find it until they harvest the corn in August."

With that, I got into the driver's seat and started the engine. Then it dawned on me what lunacy this was. We were hijacking NBC's remote truck. Before we left the scene of the almost crime, Wussler took out his handkerchief and wiped our fingerprints off the keys. It was maybe the nuttiest thing either of us ever did, but the competition between CBS and NBC was so fierce even in 1959 that for a moment, at least, it seemed like the thing to do.

When I got to Iowa I did what I always do when I get to a strange town. I went looking for someone who could show me around, could open doors and point me in the right direction. So, I made an appointment with the chief of police and asked him if he had an off-duty cop available who might want to be the CBS driver for the next couple of days. He said he hadn't, but why didn't I try the ex-chief, who had just retired and knew the town better than anyone. He got him on the phone and we made a deal contingent on the new chief letting the old chief wear the chief's uniform he had just put away in the closet.

Now we were set. There wasn't anywhere we couldn't go. Who was going to stop anyone riding with the chief? But what to do when he wasn't with us?

"I know," the chief said, "we'll make you an honorary sheriff." The next day, wearing my new Stetson and my new gold badge, I went out to the Garst farm again. The NBC remote truck was now in place and the crew was busy setting up their cameras for the big event the next day. I sauntered over. The crew had been sent out from Omaha, and hadn't the slightest idea who I was.

"Morning, Sheriff," one of them said.

"Morning, boys," I said. "What's goin' on?"

"Come on, we'll show you," one of the NBC cameramen said. He pointed toward a hayloft and said, "We got a camera up there and CBS doesn't know about it."

I excused myself, saying I had to make a call, and as I wandered by the CBS truck, told my guys, "Get a camera up in the hayloft."

Then I strolled back to the NBC truck.

"You know what else we got that CBS doesn't know about?" another cameraman said.

"What's that, young feller?" I said.

"We got a camera hidden in the pigpen," he said. I strolled past the CBS truck again. "Put a camera in the pigpen," I said.

About that time, one of the NBC directors from New York arrived and recognized me, and the jig was up.

When I got back to the hotel I had a message to call my boss in New York.

"We've had a complaint about you," he said. "NBC is charging you with impersonating a police officer."

"Not so," I said. "I'm not impersonating anything. I'm an honorary sheriff and I've got the hat and badge to prove it."

A Little Town in Jersey

There was also the time Alexei Kosygin, Premier of the USSR, came to the U.N. and wanted to meet with Lyndon Johnson while he was here. Perish the thought that a big Russian bear like Kosygin should go to Washington to call on the President. And perish the thought that a big Texas bull like LBJ should come to New York to call on a Russian. Did they draw straws or toss a coin? No. They went to a map—probably a map like the one you get in gas stations—and found a town halfway between Washington and New York where they could meet with neither of them losing face.

It was just before 7:00 P.M. when the office called. "Get to Glassboro, New Jersey, as fast as you can."

"What happened? A plane crash?" I asked.

"No, that's where Johnson and Kosygin are going to meet."

"Glassboro, New Jersey? You're kidding," I said.

"No, I'm not. There's a college in that town and they're going to meet in the college president's house."

Finding the town wasn't easy, but shortly after coming out of the Lincoln Tunnel that connects Manhattan with New Jersey, I spotted a convoy of telephone trucks heading south and I figured they must be on their way to install communications equipment. Following them turned out to be the way to Glassboro.

The next morning everybody hit upon the same idea. The lawn of the house across the street from the college president's house was the best vantage point. It was up on a little bluff, and from there you could peek into the garden where the two leaders were sure to stroll during recesses in their meetings. We were all setting up there on the lawn—CBS, NBC and ABC—each one trying to build a higher camera platform than the next. There had to be a way around this one, and there was. I went around to the back door of the house.

"Excuse me, sir," I said, "but do you own this house?"

"Yes," the man said.

"Want to rent it for the next couple of days?"

"Rent it? Where would we live?"

"Right here," I said. "You can go on living in it and I'll pay you $150 a day if you just sign a paper leasing it to me. You don't have to move out." We drew up the lease on his kitchen table.

"Okay, what now?" he said.

"Now," I said, "please go out and tell ABC and NBC to get off my lawn." He did. He told them he had rented the house to CBS and that if need be, he would call the cops. I was not the most popular man in Glassboro, but I got the best pictures.

HARRY REASONER:
That's a repetitive theme in [Chancellor Helmut] Schmidt's private and public talk—that there is no world leadership role for Germany. Why? Privately he says, "It is because we are the nation of Auschwitz . . ."
Is there any chance at all that Germany would ever again become a threat to peace?

SCHMIDT:
I am convinced that there is no chance for such a development . . . Never again will a war in Europe originate from German soil, [though] it cannot be excluded for us Germans that we might be dragged into wars that start at some other place . . .

REASONER:
But you won't start it again?

SCHMIDT:
Certainly not, sir. I've had enough. Haven't you?

WILLIAM F. BUCKLEY, JR.
January 18, 1981

MORLEY SAFER:
There's a fair body of opinion in this country . . . of people who may not regard themselves as liberals, [yet who] see conservatism as something fairly sinister. Any grounds for that sort of feeling at all?

BUCKLEY:
No. No. They—they are indulging in a false lazy historial disjunction that saw Hitler as the arch-conservative. Conservatism begins by saying you must not trifle with the individual. The best friend of individual freedom is the conservative. And if . . . the Moral Majority or the John Birch Society, or whatever, were actually to threaten the United States with oppression, you would find an instantly galvanized body of conservative opinion opposing them.

MIKE WALLACE:
Jimmy, who was the first person you killed?

FRATIANNO:
Frankie Nicoli.

WALLACE:
Where did you kill him?

FRATIANNO:
In my house. We strangled him.

WALLACE:
You were a good killer?

FRATIANNO:
I just had the talent to do things like that . . . Just some people are a little better [at it] than others.

"THE LAST MAFIOSO"

In the fall of 1980 when Mike Wallace and one of our producers, Marion Goldin, told me they wanted to do a story on fratianno, I said what in hell is fratianno? It sounded to me like an Italian dish or something consenting adults do to each other.

It turned out that fratianno was not a thing but a he—Jimmy Fratianno, better known as Jimmy "Weasel" Fratianno, who, Mike told me, was ready to tell us what he had told the government about his life in the Mob—including a story about Frank Sinatra allegedly wanting to have some guy's legs broken.

Here we go again, I thought. Fifteen years before, I had produced a documentary on Sinatra and he was still sore at me because of questions Walter Cronkite had asked him in that documentary about gambling and the Mob.

A Better Part of a Year With Old Blue Eyes

My acquaintanceship with Frank Sinatra—it was never a friendship—began in early 1965 when Sinatra's press agent, Jim Mahoney, who now handles Bob Hope, Jack Lemmon and Johnny Carson, among others, took me to Sinatra's office. Jim and I had agreed earlier that old blue eyes came as close as anyone to being show biz's Renaissance man. Movies, records, personal appearances for money, personal appearances for charity; you name it, he did it.

Jim knew the sale had already been made, but I didn't, so I was selling like crazy. Sinatra, who had already made up his mind to do the documentary, figured he'd needle me a little to find out what kind of a guy I was. Mahoney says he can't recall precisely who said what to whom, but he says my recollection that it went, more or less, like this isn't far off.

"Frank, this is Don Hewitt," Mahoney said.

"Hello, Don, what's on your mind," Sinatra said.

"I want to do a documentary about you."

"Why?"

"Because, like Jonas Salk and Hubert Humphrey and Joe DiMaggio, you are part of the times in which we live." God, how I was selling. "You're part of the fabric of the fifties and sixties. People I grew up with remember who they were with and where they were by which Frank Sinatra song was popular at the time." Andy Rooney gave me that line. Sinatra warmed up a little. I thought I was doing great. Then he asked, "What's in it for me?"

I wasn't prepared for that one and it called for some fancy footwork. "Let's face it," I said. "You haven't got enough money to buy a CBS News documentary on yourself. CBS News doesn't have enough money to pay you what you're worth. Let's call it a wash." What I didn't know was that "What's in it for me?" didn't mean money.

"How do I know I can trust you?" came next.

"Frank," I said, "I'm going to ask you to sit in a seat opposite Walter Cronkite. That's the same seat that Dwight Eisenhower, Jack Kennedy and Lyndon Johnson sat in. If you don't think you're big enough to sit in that seat, I wouldn't do it if I were you."

He grinned and said, "I'm recording tomorrow night. Want to start then?"

We did. It was the night he recorded "It Was a Very Good Year" for his *September of My Years* album.

I'd heard that he was difficult, but that night he couldn't have been more cooperative. Frank Sinatra was playing "Frank Sinatra" . . . the man on the album cover. I wish the rest had been as easy. It turned out to be a bitch.

Before we started filming other sequences, Sinatra's attorney, Mickey Rudin, flew to New York to set up some ground rules: what we could ask and what we couldn't—specifically, no questions about Cal-Neva Lodge, the Las Vegas casino Sinatra had an interest in. Rudin had lunch in the CBS cafeteria with me and Fred Friendly. No way, Friendly said, could we or would we agree to any ground rules. Either Sinatra would do it no-holds-barred or we weren't interested. Rudin said that unless we agreed to steer clear of those areas Sinatra wasn't interested. So it stunned me when Mahoney called a few days later and gave me a list of things Sinatra would be doing that we could film. My guess is that Rudin had gone back and told Sinatra that we had agreed to his ground rules because several months into the shooting, during a lull in the interview with Cronkite, Sinatra called me into the next room and told me that I had broken all the rules.

"What rules?" I asked him.

"Mickey's rules," he said.

"We never agreed to those," I told him, but he didn't seem to believe it, and from that moment on, he marked me as a bad guy. We never spoke again.

Up to that point it had been more or less smooth sailing. We had arrived at Sinatra's Palm Springs house early the previous morning to set up for the interview. With me was David Buksbaum, an associate producer then, a CBS vice president now; and Andy Rooney, a damned good writer then, a damned good writer now. Sinatra, we were told, would not be arriving until late that night and please go ahead and set up your cameras. Boy, did we set up. We rolled up the rugs, arranged and rearranged the furniture while our cameraman Wade Bingham strung cables every which way and planted lights where chairs and end tables used to be.

In the kitchen, studiously ignoring the mess in the living room, was Sinatra's main man, George Jacobs, a young, good-looking black guy who tripled as cook, valet and butler. While he prepared lunch he regaled us with Sinatra stories including one about the time in Hawaii, he said, when Mr. S., displeased with some spaghetti he had cooked, called him out of the kitchen and before all the dinner guests asked him, "What's this shit?," and dumped the whole mess of it over his head.

Another time, Jacobs told us, Sinatra was unhappy with the way he had stowed the luggage on a private jet going from London to Paris or vice versa and told someone, his pal Jilly Rizzo, I think, to open the door and throw George out as they were flying over the English Channel.

I don't think George thought he was telling tales out of school. I think he

thought those stories were part of the Sinatra folklore.

When Sinatra arrived at the house after midnight, he couldn't believe what we had done to his living room. Lucky for me he didn't say, "What's this shit?" and dump the mess over my head. What he did say was, "I shot *The Pride and the Passion* with less lights than these." To which Rooney replied, "Yeah, but this is going to be a better picture." It was.

Before the Palm Springs interview, and before Sinatra and I stopped talking, or more accurately before he stopped talking to me, he and Mia Farrow (to whom he was then engaged) had been together on a yacht anchored in New York's Hudson River. It was no surprise that everyone wanted pictures of them. It was also no surprise that Sinatra wanted none of it. One of those who tried to get aboard but didn't was a tall blond reporter for WCBS-TV named Jeanne Parr, who ended her story about Frank and Mia noting indignantly: "They're not even married." The next morning the CBS operator called me at home and said, "I have Frank Sinatra on the line."

"Put him through," I said.

Without even a hello, the voice that purred to millions "I've Got a Crush on You, Sweetie Pie," purred to me, "You got a cunt named Jeanne Parr working for you?"

It was not as alliterative as "You're dead; you're all . . . dead, dead, dead," which Barbara Howar of *Entertainment Tonight* says he purred to her, or as classy as "You scum, go home and take a bath. Here's two dollars, baby, that's what you're worth," which Maxine Cheshire, then of the Washington *Post,* said he purred to her, but as bons mots go, it wasn't bad.

"Doesn't work for me, Frank," I said.

Then to cool him down, I said, "Hey, Frank, you know what I heard yesterday? I heard NBC wants you for a musical special."

"Yeah?" he said. "They got a million dollars?"

"I hear they got five hundred thousand."

"I got more than that on me," he said.

He might have had. As Cronkite said about Sinatra in our broadcast, "The proceeds from the ballad 'Young at Heart' alone would provide a luxurious life income for most men." Arguable, but remember, that was twenty years ago. What you can't argue with, even today, is, as Cronkite also said, "people who know music hear sounds no one else makes when Sinatra sings."

Now, fifteen years after we aired that broadcast, Mike was proposing a story on another singer who also made sounds "no one else makes." Only this guy was doing his singing to the Feds, and one of the people he was singing about was Frank Sinatra.

What the hell, I said to Mike, let's do it!

WALLACE: Jimmy fought his way through the ghetto streets of Cleveland, where a policeman first labeled him "a weasel." He served seven years for armed robbery, the first of almost twenty years he would spend in prison. Shortly after his first release he moved to California and in a ceremony marked by gun and sword, he became a "made" member of the Mafia.

FRATIANNO: There's a gun and a sword crossing one another. The boss says something in Italian. We all hold hands. Manna ta ka [?] That means you're tying each other's hands. They prick your finger with a sword or with a pin to draw blood. And you go around and meet everybody and you kiss 'em on the cheek. Now you're a made member.

WALLACE: What are the privileges? What are the responsibilities of a made member of the Cosa Nostra?

FRATIANNO: Well, most people get made because they want respect.

WALLACE: Respect from whom?

FRATIANNO: Well, respect when you go to another town, they send you to the boss and they take you around. They take care of your hotel and you meet a nice class of people.

WALLACE: You meet a nice class of people! You meet some other mobsters?

FRATIANNO: Well, you also meet nice people. I met George Raft. I met a lot of—years ago, Milton Berle, Ben Blue. I know many a times I went to Vegas; where nobody could get a seat I got a front seat because I was Jimmy Fratianno.

WALLACE: Fratianno says Sinatra wanted to meet him because Sinatra knew Fratianno called the shots in California and because he wanted a favor from Jimmy. Fratianno says Jilly Rizzo, Sinatra's good friend, told him Sinatra wanted something done about his former bodyguard, Banjo Celemtano.

FRATIANNO: Jilly Rizzo told me that Frank wanted the legs broke of some guy that was writing a story about him in a paper or in a book.

WALLACE: And why would Sinatra want Celemtano's legs broken, allegedly?

FRATIANNO: Jilly told me that he put something in a book or was going to write a book or something like that.

WALLACE: Did you ever break his legs?

FRATIANNO: No. We couldn't find him.

WALLACE: When we contacted Rizzo he would neither confirm nor deny that report. Sinatra and his representatives never responded to our inquiries.

MORLEY SAFER:
His proper name is Walter Wellesley Smith, but you'd have to be even older than he is to recall reading that by-line. Red Smith is the quiet man of sports journalism, and, yet, the keenest of all the observers of the games people play.

What is it about sports that makes everyone an expert?

SMITH:
It doesn't take a monumental brain to understand that three strikes are out . . . Frank Graham used to say, when there'd be a dispute over the point system in judging a close fight, he'd say, "Bring a six-year-old kid in. Let him sit at ringside and, when it's over, say, 'who won?' And he'll say, 'He did!'"

HARRY REASONER:
Eugene Accas is vice president for network relations at the Leo Burnett advertising agency.
When you discuss what [TV shows] you want to buy, does anything moral ever enter in about elevating the taste of the public or improving the quality of television?

ACCAS:
I have to stop you. We have to establish a definition of American commercial television. It is not an instrument to raise the cultural level of appreciation of the American public. It is not an educational medium. It is a medium of mass entertainment and information, run for a profit and fueled by advertising dollars.

REASONER:
Is this good?

ACCAS:
It just is.

BRADLEY
REASONER
SAFER
WALLACE

I was addressing a meeting of the CBS Black Employee's Association the day I got the word that the powers-that-be had agreed that Ed Bradley should be Dan Rather's replacement on *60 Minutes.* So, I decided to drop that tidbit, and it started a wave of applause.

"Hold it, hold it," I said. "You don't understand. Bradley would have gotten the job even if he had been white." He's so good and so savvy and so lights up the tube every time he's on it that I wonder what took us so long. So does Mike, who had cornered Bradley in the Century Plaza Hotel several years before at the 1978 meeting of CBS affiliated stations and . . . well, let Ed tell it:

> At the time I was covering the White House and anchoring the CBS Sunday Night News. I had worked with Wallace at the Republican Convention in 1976 and had marveled at his persistence in going after delegates in search of a story on the floor of the Kemper Arena. But I wasn't prepared for Wallace going after me. He peppered me with questions—most of them prefaced with, "Listen, kid . . ."
>
> At first I had no idea what he was talking about. But, even someone as removed from the politics and rumor mill of CBS News as I was could figure it out.
>
> A decision had been made to add a fourth correspondent to *60 Minutes.* And it had pretty much boiled down to a choice between Harry Reasoner and myself, and Wallace wanted to know how I would fit in.
>
> The way I looked at it I was in a no-lose situation. I either went to *60 Minutes* or I replaced Harry at *CBS Reports.* I had always wanted to do documentaries and was not at all disappointed when Harry was named the fourth reporter at *60 Minutes* and I went to *CBS Reports.*
>
> Two years later the big guessing game around CBS was who will replace Cronkite? Rather or Mudd? When Dan got the nod, Roger got a deal: as much time off with pay as he needed to speculate about his future.
>
> About that other guessing game: who would replace Rather on *60 Minutes,* it soon became apparent that I was the front runner, if I believed Hewitt, who went around saying to everybody but me, "If there's a better reporter than Bradley, I wish someone would point him out," but still he never said it to me. Finally I was in Los Angeles again, this time for a Q and A session with the TV critics, when a reporter in the back of the room, sick of hearing about what a great deal Mudd got, asked Bob Chandler, the CBS News vice president who looked after *60 Minutes,* about who was going to replace Rather. Either Chandler was writing Hewitt's lines or Hewitt was writing his: "If there is a better reporter than Bradley, etc. . . ." was the answer.
>
> Next, a reporter who remembered my being runner-up to Harry two years earlier asked what I would do if I was passed over again. I said, "I'd like to have the same kind of deal Roger Mudd got." I got an even better deal. The next week I was named to replace Dan Rather.

THE WAY *60 MINUTES* WORKS

Shortly after Ed Bradley joined *60 Minutes,* my secretary, Beverly Morgan, came into my office, closed the door behind her, and said, "I think you should see this."

It was a copy of a memo from Bradley to CBS personnel informing them that he had formally changed his name from Ed Bradley to Shaheeb Sha Hab, and that from now on he wanted all his records to reflect the fact that he had taken a Muslim name.

Wow, this was a tough one. You can't tell a man he can't change his name, especially if he is doing it for religious reasons, but all I could hear at that moment was: "I'm Mike Wallace. I'm Morley Safer. I'm Harry Reasoner. I'm Shaheeb Sha Hab; those stories and Andy Rooney tonight on *60 Minutes.*"

"Is he kidding?" I asked Beverly.

"I don't think so," she said. "The memo has already gone to personnel."

I decided to find out if it was on the level. "I think I know how to smoke him out," I said. I went into Bradley's office, memo in hand, and told him that I admired what he was doing and that I thought we should call the television columnists and wire services and give them the story.

"Good idea," Bradley said. "Do you want to call them or do you want me to?"

"Why don't I do it?" I said.

"Fine and dandy," Ed said. "You do it."

My God, I thought. He isn't bluffing. I picked up the phone and dialed United Press International. As I waited for them to answer, I kept staring at Bradley.

"Hello," I said, when they did. "I think I have an item for you."

That's when Bradley hollered uncle. "Hang up," he said. "Tell him you'll call back."

Among other things, it's fun being the executive producer of *60 Minutes.* But what in hell does it *mean* to be the executive producer of *60 Minutes*?

For starters, it doesn't mean that you own it. Sometimes TV producers do own their shows—but not news shows. For instance, my friend Mark Goodson, who owns quiz shows, is a real television producer. The same with my friend Norman Lear, who owns sitcoms, and in the sixties and seventies, along with Grant Tinker, now the president of NBC, produced almost every one of them worth producing.

By those standards, I'm not a producer. Producing, in my end of television, simply means that you are the one in charge, although there are always assorted vice presidents looking over your shoulder. Everybody, it seems, wants to be a producer. Even vice presidents want to be producers.

Before I became a producer, the job I was hired to fill in 1949 was that of associate director. The director I was hired to "associate" with was not a real director like the ones in Hollywood, but a kind of traffic cop presiding over an electronic intersection called the control room. What he did and what I helped him do was to make sure the film came in on cue and the graphics came up when they were supposed to and that nothing bumped into anything else and that when Doug Edwards said, "Now a word from Oldsmobile," that's what you got, and not a report from Washington. Thirty-seven years later it's pretty much the same, although the traffic is much heavier and it comes into the control room every which way, including down from satellites orbiting overhead.

But what directing in my end of television *doesn't* mean is that you tell Walter Cronkite or Dan Rather or Mike Wallace how to broadcast. It only means that you tell them where to sit and which camera to look at and when to start and when to stop, though if the director of a news show is really good, like Arthur Bloom, who directs *60 Minutes* and all the big events like the political conventions and election nights, he helps shape the entire look and feel and sound of the broadcast. (Sometimes Artie acts even goofier than I do. When he wanted to put a camera over the podium at the 1984 Democratic Convention in San Francisco, he was told he couldn't because in the event of an earthquake the camera might come down and kill someone. "I'll take the chance," he said. You see, it's not just the delegates who go ape at conventions.)

How do I produce *60 Minutes*? Principally, without meetings and memos. I have always believed that if we held meetings, we would look like a meeting, and if we wrote memos, we would look like a memo, although we did have a meeting back in 1972. It's a very loose shop, run on an open door policy—literally an open door policy. I don't remember the last time I closed my office door. When Mike gets an idea he bursts into my office with a "Hey, kid, why don't we . . ." Or Morley comes in with a "Did you see the story about . . . ?" Or Harry walks in and says, "Isn't it about time we did . . . ?" Or Ed is curious about "How come we're not looking into . . . ?" Or Diane will say, "Have you thought about . . . ?" Or one of the producers comes in with an idea. Each of the correspondents has a team of four producers and one associate producer. And there are two more who go from correspondent to correspondent, working with whoever doesn't have a full plate at the moment, and then there's the senior producer, Phil Scheffler, and before him, Palmer Williams. Four of

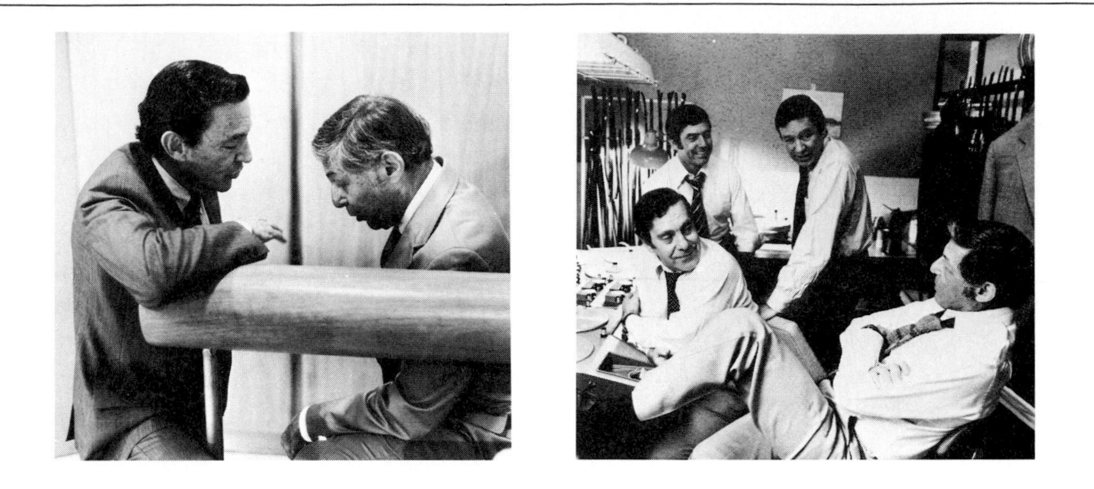

the producers are based in Washington, three in London, one in Paris, one in San Francisco, and the rest are in New York. So story ideas come from all over. Every one of us calls on everything we have read about or heard about to help us make up the budget of one hundred or so stories we report every year. A lot are sparked by suggestions sent in by viewers.

After talking an idea over with Phil or me, one of the correspondents or one of the producers writes up what we call a "blue sheet" with an outline of the story (the blue sheets are white, but they used to be on blue paper, hence the name). Just because someone else has already done a story is no reason to reject it if we think we can add a new dimension or tell it better. Sometimes what others see as only a local story, a *60 Minutes* producer sees in a larger context and figures out an angle to make it of interest to everyone. For instance, Norman Gorin, one of our long-time producers, came to Morley Safer with a story that ran in the Milwaukee *Sentinel* about two cops who, twenty years before, had killed a young black kid who pulled a knife on them. Now one of the cops had come forward and said that the kid was unarmed, that after he and his partner had killed him they had planted a knife on him, and the thought of it had ruined his life. All of a sudden a local crime became bigger than just a Milwaukee story. As Gorin and Safer saw it, the cop could have been any cop, the kid any kid, and the place any place. We called the story "The Cop, the Kid and the Knife."

After Scheffler and I approve a blue sheet, it goes to our boss (first Bill Leonard, then Bob Chandler, then Roger Coloff, and now Eric Ober), who evaluates it in the light of other stories done by the Evening News or *CBS Reports*, or Sunday Morning, etc. When he sends it back with his okay, things begin to happen. The research begins. The producer goes out on location to size up the story, keeping in phone contact almost every day with his correspondent and usually with Phil Scheffler. Once the producer begins to get a fix on the situation, the shape of the story may change. The woman who sounded so good in print turns out to be a dodo, but the woman across the street is sensational. The story really isn't exactly what we had been led to

believe, but there is an even better story in the next town. The mayor who had been so forthcoming in print clams up when he sees a camera. "Do you still think there's a story?" Phil or I might ask the producer. Sometimes the producer says, "Sure there is, but it's not exactly the one we thought there was."

"Okay," we usually tell him, "talk to Mike (or Morley or Harry or Ed or Diane) and see if he (or she) is still interested." If he is, the producer keeps going, and when he has all his ducks in a row he sends for the correspondent, who goes over the story with him, meets the people involved, reads whatever it is the producer thinks is important and then goes to work with a camera and mike. Because each producer turns out about five stories apiece and the correspondent turns out twenty, it stands to reason that the producer will spend more time on an individual story than the correspondent. That's why we feature each producer's name on the screen. To us it's what a double by-line is to a newspaper. Both producer and correspondent worked on the story and both of them will work on the editing.

Let me stop here for a moment and go back to something I touched on earlier. The title of producer in my business is a misnomer. If I could get rid of it, I would. I think of the entire *60 Minutes* staff as reporters and editors—the so-called producers and the correspondents. They all report, they all edit, but the correspondents broadcast better than the others, so we use them to tell the story on the air.

How do we decide what to put on each week? We go to the blackboard. It's a blackboard just like the one you remember from school. Up on the board are five columns headed "Wallace," "Safer," "Reasoner," "Bradley" and "Sawyer." In chalk is the working title of a story each is working on. When the story has been completed to the satisfaction of the producer and the correspondent, it is shown to me and Scheffler and our boss. If it "passes," it gets a number, which is its exact running time. Then it's put on the shelf as a candidate for a future *60 Minutes* broadcast.

When the blackboard is full—six stories apiece with running times next to them for a total of thirty is a number I like—I can look up at the board on a Monday morning and say, "That Wallace story, that Safer story and that Reasoner story will make a good show." Or, "That Wallace story is too long to go with that Safer story, but if we substitute another Safer story and add a short Bradley piece rather than a longer Sawyer story, it'll be a better show and leave us time for two minutes of Rooney and about a minute and a half of mail."

Having a full board is the key. Having enough stories ready to go gives you the luxury of making up the best mix and not having to go with something half-baked because there is nothing else ready.

The week before each broadcast I go over each story and extract from it a thirty-second excerpt to put at the beginning of the broadcast to attract attention. Murrow used to tell a story about a farmer who sold another farmer a mule and told him all he had to do was talk nicely to the mule and he would do anything the farmer wanted him to.

A day later, driving past the home of the farmer to whom he had sold the mule, the first farmer saw the man out in his front yard hitting the mule in the head with a sledgehammer. "What are you doing?" he asked. "I told you all you had to do was talk nicely to him."

"I know," the second farmer said, "but first I have to get his attention, don't I?"

That's what I figure: First I have to get their attention, don't I?

Is that it? Almost, but not quite. There are a marvelous bunch of film and tape editors—one for each producer—headed by Ken Dalglish, who makes sure that the editing process is keeping pace with the needs of the show and that his team of twenty-two is turning out stories fast enough to keep that blackboard filled. They are the best in the business. So is our sound technician Joel Dullberg.

I am a bug on audio, convinced that it is your ear as much as your eye that keeps you glued to a television set. I am also a bug on writing and delivery. I will frequently tell a correspondent that a pause is too long, or not long enough, or that an inflection is wrong. Is that dramatic coaching? No, that's editing. Inflections and pauses are to us what commas and semicolons are to print people.

What do I do besides that? I'm a busybody, making suggestions to a producer and to his or her editor. "If you change the middle, the viewer might get a picture

of . . ." or, "I think you might do better to change the opening so it reflects . . ." or, "Have you thought of using the closing sequence higher up to . . ."

Do they resent my butting in? As long as they feel free to tell me they think I'm wrong, I don't think they mind. It's from that kind of give and take that *60 Minutes* gets on the air. It's that rubbing against one another that generates psychic energy. If we have been successful, I think it's because we are able to transmit that psychic energy through the tube every Sunday night at seven.

When people ask me, as they do, "How long in advance do you produce the show?," I usually tell them, "You don't understand. We don't produce a show. We produce stories, and once a week we assemble three of them into a show." Assembling the stories into a show is the easiest thing we do. We simply make the trek every Friday morning from our offices in another building to the CBS Broadcast Center and put the correspondents in front of a camera with a magazine page electronically displayed behind them. Then we insert the stopwatch and the commercials and the station breaks, and by Friday afternoon another broadcast is in the can—though we can open it up for a late development right up to 7:00 P.M. on Sunday, and have.

Why hasn't anyone duplicated our success? The answer is that duplicating *60 Minutes* is like duplicating *All in the Family*. It's as if some television exec wrote a memo to his staff saying that *All in the Family* was a big success so why don't we also do a show about a loveable loud mouth who calls his wife a dingbat and his son-in-law a meathead. Terrific idea. If you've got Carroll O'Connor, Jean Stapleton, Sally Struthers, Rob Reiner and Norman Lear, you've got a hit. If you don't, you know what you've got? You've got a memo. Without Mike Wallace, Morley Safer, Dan Rather, Harry Reasoner, Ed Bradley, Diane Sawyer and the great producers and film and tape editors we've got, that's what *60 Minutes* would still be—a memo.

CBS is the only network with enough bench strength to peel off a Wallace, a Safer, a Reasoner, a Bradley, and a Sawyer, and twenty-two of the best producers in the business and assign them exclusively to one broadcast, and have left over a Dan Rather, a Charles Kuralt, a Bill Moyers, a Leslie Stahl, a Tom Fenton, a Bruce Morton, a Bob Simon and a Bob Schieffer. Who else but CBS can do that?

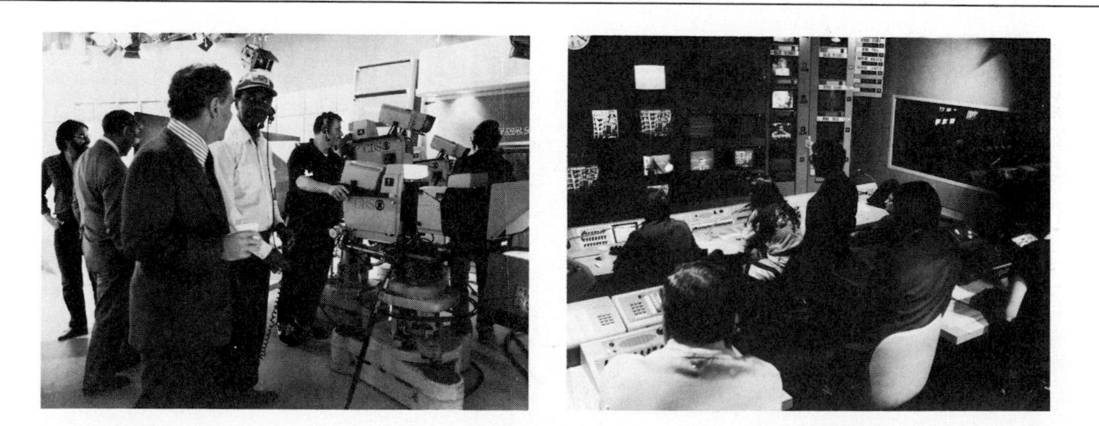

IRA
November 4, 1981

"THE OTHER FACE OF THE IRA"

ED BRADLEY: It might seem that Libya's Colonel Qaddafi and certain members of the Irish American community in the United States would make strange bedfellows, but bedfellows they are, as joint suppliers of illegal weapons to the IRA. Over the years, most of the weapons captured by security forces in Northern Ireland have been of American manufacture, smuggled directly from the United States, but now there is increasing evidence that more and more of the incoming hardware is of Soviet origin . . .

POLICE OFFICER: They are the AK-47's—

BRADLEY: Kalashnikovs . . .

POLICE OFFICER: —Kalashnikovs, and they are standard Eastern-bloc weapons . . .

BRADLEY: Is this change from American-made to Eastern-bloc weapons just a coincidence? Not according to Peter McMullen, . . . [who] was a top soldier with the IRA from 1971 to 1978. He planted bombs and led sniper patrols. He was jailed by the British, but now he's on the run in the United States, seeking political asylum. McMullen says he's been sentenced to death by the IRA, because he disagreed with their political direction and wanted out.

McMULLEN: They had turned very strongly toward socialism. They had started to get involved with other groups—Baader-Meinhof, the Red Brigades, PLO—and a lot of the individual members' thinking was that we're not having an Irish revolution anymore, we're having a world revolution. . .

BRADLEY: Why would Qaddafi support the IRA?

McMULLEN: Qaddafi supports all revolutions, and that's what the IRA has become now—a revolution.

BRADLEY: A Socialist revolution?

McMULLEN: A Socialist revolution. . .

BRADLEY: Socialist thinking has usually been associated with radical universities, but the IRA has very few college-educated members.

McMULLEN: Jail is the greatest university in the world for soldiers.

BRADLEY: And what are they exposed to in jail? . . . What kind of teaching?

McMULLEN: Well, reading mostly . . .

BRADLEY: Marx? Lenin?

McMULLEN: Lenin, Che Guevara, Castro—it's just a progression . . .

BRADLEY: You know, there—there are a lot of people in this country who'd find that hard to believe.

McMULLEN: A—a lot of people in Ireland would find it hard to believe, too, but unfortunately, it's true.

BRADLEY: Claire Sterling is an American journalist who has lived some thirty years in Italy. She is best known for her expertise on terrorist groups, and her latest book charts the links among many of the world's terrorist organizations. The group you know best, I guess then, would be, what, the Red Brigades? . . . Do you see any connection between the Red Brigades and the IRA?

STERLING: Oh, certainly. There's a very close connection. There has been all during the seventies . . .

BRADLEY: The IRA was the oldest guerrilla force in Europe, going back fifty years, but the IRA that we hear about today is a splinter group that broke away in 1969 and called itself the Provisional IRA.

How soon did they become involved with other European terrorist groups?

STERLING: Well, they began that very year. The first Provos went for training to Lebanon, to Palestinian camps in Lebanon, in 1969 . . .

BRADLEY: Perhaps the best known of the Irish figures in this country is Bernadette Devlin McAliskey. While not a member of the IRA, she is the spokesperson for the H-Block committee, which represents the IRA hunger strikers . . .

Do you practice a religion?

McALISKEY: Oh, I'm an expert.

BRADLEY: I mean, do you go to church?

McALISKEY: Oh, that's none of your business.

BRADLEY: Do you have a formal religion? Is that my business?

McALISKEY: No. I don't ask you.

BRADLEY: I'd tell you, if you asked.

McALISKEY: I am not interested. It's none of my business.

BRADLEY: Well, I'm interested in you. That's why I ask.

McALISKEY: It's none of your business.

BRADLEY: Well now—are you a Socialist? Are you a Marxist?

McALISKEY: Yes, I'm a Socialist.

BRADLEY: Are you a Leninist? Or what?

McALISKEY: People say I'm a Trot.

BRADLEY: Trotskyite?

McALISKEY: A Trotskyite, if you don't like them, and a Trotskyist if you do.

BRADLEY: Ah!

McALISKEY: People say I'm a Trot.

BRADLEY: Are you?

McALISKEY: I've never read enough of Trotsky to know what, exactly, the man thinks and whether he agrees with me or not . . .

BRADLEY: Catholics mourn the hunger strikers as heroes fallen in the struggle for a united Ireland, but this emotional support for the IRA has never been expressed as political support at the polls. In the Catholic South, out of more than 500 council seats, only 30 members are supporters; and in the British Parliament, they hold only one of 12 seats representing the North . . .

McMULLEN: The thinking was that when we finish the war in the North, then we've got to fight it in the South, you know, against the—the Southern politicians, and the setup they have down there.

BRADLEY: Do you think that . . . Marxist views would be acceptable to the majority of Catholics in the North or the South?

McMULLEN: No, definitely not.

McALISKEY: At the end of the day, God will be on the side of the winner, regardless of who wins, regardless of how he wins, because God always was and always will be. And that's how He's figured it out. That's how God always was and that's how God always will be. Because without political principle or anything else, as long as you keep going home with a winner, you'll last forever. So all we have to do is win. No doubt.

BRADLEY: Then God will be on your side.

McALISKEY: Our God will be on our side.

It was not a story to gladden the hearts of veterans of the Irish wars against the British, many of whom live in the United States. Could it be that the army they and their fathers had served had joined hands with the Red Brigades, and that their nephews and nieces back in Ireland were reading Che Guevara and Lenin? They didn't want to believe it any more than they wanted to believe that the heroine of the Belfast barricades, Bernadette Devlin McAliskey, had actually told Ed Bradley: "God will be on the side of the winner, regardless of who wins, regardless of how he wins . . . That's how God always was and that's how God always will be." But she said it on a Sunday night in some thirty million American living rooms, and once they had seen it, a lot of IRA supporters became former supporters.

ED BRADLEY:
"When I was a boy," Izzy Stone once wrote, "I believed that a newspaperman ought to use his power on behalf of those who were getting the dirty end of the deal." He is seventy-three and retired now . . . There is no more *I. F. Stone's Weekly,* but there is still I. F. Stone. How do you feel about [Ronald Reagan]?

STONE:
I think he's an awfully nice guy, but he scares the hell out of me . . . His premise is that all you've got to do is unleash greed. You know, when you come to town with a $50 haircut and a thousand-dollar suit, with all these rich friends who . . . import hairdressers and couturiers and cooks for their big parties, and you tell the poor, "Hey, times are bad, folks, you've got to pull in your belt." And the poor sucker that can't afford a forty-nine-cent cup of coffee for lunch . . . has to pull in his belt .

PALERMO
December 13, 1981

"WELCOME TO PALERMO"

HARRY REASONER: In one six-day period while we were in Palermo, they played the same scene nine times. When the police got where they were going, they always found another victim of the war among the Mafia. Giacomo Tafuri got it at high noon on the street, but predictably no one could remember noticing who shot him: twice in the chest, followed by the ritual *coup de grâce*—three bullets in the head. Tafuri was on the police books for narcotics activities. An agent of the United States Drug Enforcement Administration, a one-time undercover man, Thomas Tripodi knows the Mafia, and Palermo.

THOMAS TRIPODI: Well, we call them murders [in the U.S.]. They are executions over there. It means the person has violated a code in the so-called Mafia. This is why they can kill a person in broad daylight, including a police officer, and [it can be] witnessed by two or three hundred people, none of whom will say anything. It's an execution, and the people know that, they understand it, because the Mafia, after all is said and done, is an underground government . . .

REASONER: Why Palermo? Look at the map. If you wanted a convenient place to stop over, with morphine base from Turkey and Lebanon and Iran and Iraq and Afghanistan; a place with clandestine laboratories to turn the morphine into heroin for the hungry addicts of Western Europe and America; if you wanted that kind of place and Palermo didn't exist, you might have to build it . . .

This is the direct New York-to-Palermo flight they call "the Mafia Express." The name is a joke, of course. These people are warm and honest first-or second-generation Americans who have saved enough dollars to come back and see a mother or a sister or some cousins. But somewhere among them are the mules, the couriers. Coming back, they may have a bundle of American cash for cousin Bruno that would choke a Sicilian donkey. Once they confiscated a suitcase from checked baggage. It had $500,000 in it. As of now, no one has ever claimed it or filed a lost luggage report . . .

[Palermo's] investigators are as smart as anybody's, but for a city the size of Washington, D.C., there are just two hundred of them. A couple of years ago, their chief had begun to have some success, to get some people charged. The Mafia shot Boris Giuliano dead as he drank a cup of coffee. [Judge] Cesare Terranova, was murdered on his way to work. The provincial president of Sicily was killed in his car after mass one Sunday. There was a courageous district attorney, Gaetano Costa. He was killed for his courage . . .

Palermo's press is also concerned. The tabloid *L'Ora,* for instance, has shown both persistence and courage in covering Mafia crimes. Its politics is left-wing. Its editor, Nicholas Cattedra, continues to investigate the Mafia even though one of his reporters was killed . . .

NICHOLAS CATTEDRA: We have investigated drugs. That's one piece. We have investigated contracts, the local council in Palermo. That's another bit. We have investigated the relations between the Mafia and politics. That's another piece. [But] if you ask me who the head of the Mafia is, I don't know. You need to go to the United States to find out . . .

REASONER: How much does it cost to get a man killed in Palermo? . . . To hire a hit man?

JUDGE MARIO SERIO: Well, I heard that someone just was satisfied with 300,000 liras, . . . which would be $300.

REASONER: Three hundred dollars.

JUDGE SERIO: Maybe a little less—$290 or so.

After we broadcast that story, a group representing the Italian-American Anti-Defamation Alliance came to call. Why, they wanted to know, did we feel it was newsworthy to shine a light on Palermo and call attention to violence.

They might have asked the same question of someone else who decided to shine a light on Palermo and call attention to the violence. His name was John Paul II and he told the world in 1982 even more explicitly than we had a year before that "the facts of barbarous violence which for too long a time have bloodied the streets of this splendid city offend human dignity."

One of the other complaints the Italian-American Anti-Defamation Alliance had was that we had thrown around the word "Mafia." You only did that, one of them told me, because it's good for ratings.

I wonder if they also told that to the Sicilian Bishops' Conference, which, after our story was on the air, excommunicated those who murder or kidnap on behalf of "the Mafia."

Did Harry Reasoner's visit to Palermo change anything? Not so we could notice. Neither, however, did the Pope's visit to Palermo. The night before he arrived in town to deplore the violence, four more people were murdered.

LENA HORNE
December 27, 1981

HORNE:
You can't help your sexual nature, you know . . . If a lady treats other people as she'd like to be treated, then she's allowed to go roll in the grass if she wants to.

ED BRADLEY:
Even if she's sixty-four?

HORNE:
Particularly if she's sixty-four!

JEANE KIRKPATRICK
January 31, 1982

KIRKPATRICK:
You know how politics is played in the Congress. . . People deal, they bargain, they . . . withhold appointments. Now, politics is played the same way in the United Nations . . . Only the United States, the Americans, who are very good at that kind of politics, are very bad at it in the United Nations.

MIKE WALLACE:
The U.N. shouldn't exist, Ambassador Kirkpatrick?

KIRKPATRICK:
Well, the U.N. does exist. You know, like death and taxes, the United Nations exists.

HARRY REASONER:

University presidents have a difficult life. They not only have to make policy and oversee the day to day operations of their schools, they also have to raise money—chiefly from the alumni. So they avoid controversy . . . Well, one university president doesn't . . . He is Father Theodore M. Hesburgh—"Hesburgh of Notre Dame."

HESBURGH:

I was discussing nuclear weapons with George Bush and I said, "George, you're a grandfather. It's like having a cobra in the nursery with your grandchildren. You don't have a big discussion about it. You get rid of the cobra or you won't have any grandchildren." . . . I keep thinking of Dante who said the worst place in hell was reserved or kept for those people who were neutral in times of great moral crises.

MORLEY SAFER:
For nearly six decades he's been the chronicler of the American theater, of American entertainment. His medium is caricature . . .

HIRSCHFELD:
I remember going to New Haven to see the thing called *Away We Go!* Lawrence Langner was the producer of that, and he asked me to have a coffee with him . . . after the show. And I did, and there was Billy Rose and Mike Todd. And the four of us were sitting at the table, and [Lawrence] said, "Now, what do you fellows think of this? I want the truth." . . . And Mike Todd, being Mike Todd, jumped into the breach and said, . . . "If it was my show, I'd close it . . . You don't have a chance. Take your lumps like a man and just forget it." And Billy said, "Wait a minute! There's a couple of tunes in there that are not bad." [Then] a press agent . . . came up to us and said, "Listen. Stay over tonight and take a look at the matinee tomorrow. We've changed the title to *Oklahoma!*, and it's not bad."

ED BRADLEY:
Acting, for Olivier is, above all, a game.

OLIVIER:
It's a game of make-believe. I mean, originally. It's just like a nursery game of make-believe. In a way the essence of it is that. I'm going to pretend I'm a fellow called Hamlet. I'm going to pretend I'm a fellow called King Lear. Lear is—I'm sorry, it's regrettably easy for me because now in my crusty old age I'm almost exactly like him. I haven't the majesty, of course, but I—I have every other characteristic of Lear: unreasonable, impossible, stupid, stubborn. And I'm sorry, that's me. In Hamlet's time, I was much more like Hamlet. I had all those qualities, all the weaknesses particularly. And I think if you can recognize that, I think that's a little secret for the actor. Use your weaknesses. Aspire to the strengths.

"LARRY"

Ed Bradley had come back to his hotel in Israel after a bad day on the West Bank (he and the crew had been stoned in an Arab village) and found a message to call Jeanne Solomon, one of the *60 Minutes* producers who works in London.

"Ed," Jeanne said, "how do you feel about stopping in London on your way home?"

"Do I have to?" Ed asked. All Ed wanted to do was finish up in Israel and get on a plane back to New York. "What do you want me for?"

"Laurence Olivier," Jeanne said.

Jeanne and Ed had been trying to get Olivier for more than two years with no success. After a while, his agents even stopped returning their calls, but now Olivier had completed his autobiography and the need to publicize a book can persuade even the most private person to do things he doesn't normally do.

Ed worried that he wouldn't have enough time to do his homework—to read up in preparation for the interview.

"Don't worry," Jeanne said. "We'll have an Olivier session when you get to London. I've got stacks and stacks of material and I've arranged for a videotape player to be in your hotel room so you can watch some cassettes of his best performances."

The interview was set for Friday. Ed arrived in London on Wednesday and for forty-eight hours, interrupted only by the room-service waiter, he boned up on Olivier. On Friday morning Jeanne picked him up and they went to Claridge's, where Jeanne had taken a suite to film the interview. Norman Langley, as good a cameraman as any in the world, was waiting, camera and lights at the ready. It got later and later. Just as Ed and Jeanne began to think Olivier had "chickened out," the door opened and in tottered a frail, elderly gentleman wearing a red-and-blue sports jacket. He looked around the room bewildered, as if he had never seen a film camera before.

Oh, Jesus, Jeanne thought. It's not going to work. She knew he had recently been ill—but could this really be the great Laurence Olivier? Jeanne knew he had just finished a television film of *King Lear*. Could Lear have finished him off? Olivier sat down and Ed began the interview—very gently. He had only gotten as far as Olivier's eighteenth birthday and some obscure story about a long-lost brother when Olivier leaned forward and said to Ed in cowboy lingo, "I'm getting tired, pardner."

Ed assured him that we were almost through. The fact is that we hadn't even begun. He agreed to stay awhile longer. Gradually, prodded by Ed's questions, the frail old man who had tottered into the room became Laurence Olivier, the actor. The interview went on for another hour and a half as Laurence Olivier and Ed Bradley jousted with each other. When Jeanne finally said "cut" neither had fallen off his horse, and we wrapped one of the more memorable *60 Minutes* interviews.

BRADLEY: Olivier says his success [in *Wuthering Heights*] was due to the director, William Wyler [Willie], who knocked him down to size. Wyler gave him such a hard time that Olivier appealed to producer Samuel Goldwyn for sympathy.

OLIVIER: Sam Goldwyn came on the stage and I thought, well, if I sort of sidle up to him, limp up to him, he's bound to say, "Willie, this poor actor! Oh, let's be on his side a little, shall we?" And as I approached him, sure enough, he held out his arm to me, like that. I thought, "Oh, God! This is working better than I ever imagined!" And he said, "Willie, if this actor goes on playing the way he is, I'll close up the picture. Will you look at that actor's ugly face? It's plain. It's dirty. It's hammy. It's stagy. I don't want a part of it. Take him away." Boy! Boy! Boy! Boy! Boy! What a stripping down was that! And from then on, I took everything Willie had to say. And out of the ashes emerged a film actor . . .

BRADLEY: Would you do anything over?

OLIVIER: I don't think so. One—was it—H. G. Wells had a wonderful line to somebody who asked him that. "Do you believe in another life, Mr. Wells?" And he said—he had a rather thin voice, and he said: "No, thank you. One life's quite enough for little old H.G." Well, I think one feels like that.

Olivier had had such a good time with *60 Minutes* that he and Ed carried on their conversation as they left the suite, went down in the elevator with their cameraman in tow and walked through the lobby of Claridge's. It ended only when the hotel manager said to Jeanne, "Madam, please remember this is a hotel not a film set." Hotels are always nervous about film cameras. Who knows when someone might inadvertently get a shot of a gentleman checking in with a lady not his wife?

Ed saw Olivier off in the Rolls-Royce we had hired to bring him to and from the interview, and went back upstairs to thank the crew for its patience, but not before telling the driver to please come back for him and Jeanne. This is one time they thought they deserved to arrive at the CBS London office in style. The Rolls came back, but as they were getting in, the car unaccountably shot forward and ricocheted off a parked Mercedes into the path of an oncoming Ford. "Gor, blimey," said the driver, "it's never done that before."

Had it done that before—only a half hour before—*60 Minutes* might have been Lawrence Olivier's last performance.

RUSSELL:
Twenty-five or thirty years ago, a player came to you as a player. Now he comes to you as a corporation.

STAUBACH:
[I deplored] the cocaine, the marijuana and the other drugs . . . I used to stare across the line of scrimmage and see a linebacker sometimes where both eyes weren't going the same way.

MIKE WALLACE:
The first producer who wanted to make her a "somebody" said that her size was against her.

HAYES:
He said, "If you were a couple of inches taller, you'd be a great star."

LENELL GETER'S
IN JAIL
December 4, 1983

"LENELL GETER'S IN JAIL"

MORLEY SAFER: Lenell Geter is a young black engineer, one of six graduates of South Carolina State College who were recruited by E-Systems, a major defense contractor, in Greenville, Texas, a small town outside of Dallas.

When he arrived there in 1982 from rural South Carolina, his future seemed secure, a clean-cut, twenty-four-year-old earning $24,000 as an engineer and planning to get married. Six months later, he was arrested for the $615 armed robbery of a Balch Springs, Texas, Kentucky Fried Chicken restaurant, convicted and sentenced to life in prison.

How did it all happen? Could Lenell Geter have been a successful engineer who went out to rob fast-food restaurants on his lunch hour or coffee breaks or after work? It all [began] with the armed robbery of [a] Kentucky Fried Chicken restaurant in Greenville, Texas, on August 9, 1982, by a young black male.

The detective investigating was Lieutenant James Fortenberry of the Greenville police. By his own admission, he was hurting for leads. So, he had the local paper appeal to anyone who'd seen any strange vehicles in the vicinity of the restaurant to contact him. Fortenberry got a call from the white woman who lived across the road from a park in Greenville. She said she'd seen a black man park his car there a number of times. She became suspicious. The car had South Carolina license plates. Now, this park is some distance from the robbery, a good three-and-a-half miles. Fortenberry considered this a major lead. He traced the license plate and the car turned out to be owned by Lennell Geter.

GETER: Well, that's my favorite reading place and place of meditating. It is a public park, and I'd usually go there and relax and feed the ducks, because it's near the water and it's comfortable. But must I be suspicious because I go to a public park and—and read? That doesn't make any sense.

SAFER: Fortenberry not only considered Geter a suspect in the Kentucky Fried Chicken robbery in Greenville, but he called the police in Plano, Texas, to tell them he might have a suspect for a similar robbery there. The Plano

police told the police in Garland, Texas, that Geter might be a suspect for a robbery there.

Well, suddenly, Geter's picture was being circulated as a suspect in robberies all over the Dallas region . . . Two weeks [later] there was a rash of three armed robberies—a Taco Bell, a mugging in a drugstore parking lot and another Kentucky Fried Chicken, this one in Balch Springs, Texas. The day after that, Lenell Geter was arrested and charged with all three robberies.

There was some talk of plea bargaining, but Geter refused, maintained he was innocent, was tried swiftly, found guilty and sentenced to life for the Kentucky Fried Chicken robbery at Balch Springs . . .

[The trial] had already begun when Geter's attorney called E-Systems and asked his co-workers to get to Dallas as quickly as possible to testify on his behalf.

Two people who were not called to testify and did not realize until after the trial that their testimony could have been crucial were Dan Walker and Debra Cotton.

DEBRA COTTON: I talked to him shortly, right around one o'clock, and then again at three, right at three.

SAFER: At three o'clock?

COTTON: Mm-hmm.

SAFER: And the robbery took place at three-twenty.

COTTON: Three-twenty.

SAFER: Absolutely impossible to get from E-Systems to Balch Springs?

COTTON: It was impossible for Lennell Geter to be there.

DAN WALKER: No question about it, he came by to use my phone, somewhere between three-forty-five and four o'clock, that afternoon.

SAFER: No way you could get back from Balch Springs in fifteen minutes?

WALKER: No. No way. No . . .

PROSECUTOR KEN CARDEN: Debra Cotton sat in this hallway throughout the trial. I never talked to her, but she had the opportunity to get on that witness stand just like any other witness and tell what she knew . . .

SAFER: You said that Debra Cotton was out here; she wasn't out here at all.

PROSECUTOR RANDY ISENBERG: There was a lady from E-Systems, I was told.

SAFER: Black or white?

ISENBERG: Black . . .

SAFER: But Debra Cotton's white.

There was no physical evidence of Geter's guilt—no gun, no cash, no license plate taken down at the scene of a crime. The State's entire case was based on eyewitness testimony.

ED SIGEL, DEFENSE LAWYER: Eyewitness testimony is subject to a great deal of error, and that's all they have—absolutely no corroborating evidence whatsoever.

SAFER: But they had five, five.

SIGEL: They had five.

SAFER: It's pretty convincing.

SIGEL: Not really, when you stop and think that each one of the persons who identified the robber described a person who doesn't even look like Geter. They have him from five-six to six-foot tall. Some of them have him with whisker hair, some of them have him with a mustache, some of them have him with long sideburns. All of them have him with the wrong hair. He never looked like that.

PROSECUTOR CARDEN: People quite often get small details incorrect in their pictures of people, the pictures they mentally retain. But when you come face to face with someone, you don't tend to forget 'em.

SAFER: But it's the small details that send a man away for life, so don't they have to be very, very carefully examined?

CARDEN: It's the live witnesses that you look at, listen to and decide after you hear them on the stand that you believe 'em that send people to the penitentiary.

SAFER: So, Geter was found guilty. Then came the punishment, the sentencing phase of the trial. The prosecution asked the jury for life for Lenell Geter, and among its witnesses was Lieutenant Fortenberry. He told the court he'd telephoned the police in South Carolina, and the sheriff down there, Sheriff Ed Darnell, had said he knew Geter and knew him to be a bad character.

Sheriff Darnell, when Lieutenant Fortenberry called you, what did he want to know about Lenell Geter?

SHERIFF ED DARNELL: He was telling me about Geter and being a suspect in this armed robbery, and said that he just needed some information on him. And I told him—I said, well, I don't have anything and I don't know him at all.

SAFER: Did you say to Lieutenant Fortenberry that if his name is Geter and he comes from Denmark, South Carolina, he must be or was probably an outlaw?

SHERIFF DARNELL: Definitely not. No, sir. No way, shape or form . . .

SAFER: There's one more thing that's important to know about the Lenell Geter story. Remember that first Kentucky Fried Chicken robbery in Greenville, the one that brought Lenell Geter into the mind of Lieutenant Fortenberry, because of that phone call he received about the out-of-state car seen at a local park? . . .

Elaine Mooney was a customer that day in the Greenville Kentucky Fried Chicken. She saw the robber. But more important, she was an employee at E-Systems and knew Lenell Geter.

ELAINE MOONEY: He was very friendly and he always called me by my name.

SAFER: So, you were on a first-name basis.

MOONEY: Yes.

SAFER: So, had that been Lenell Geter in there holding up that restaurant . . .

MOONEY: I think he would have said hello. And I don't think he would have continued on to rob, if I'd seen him.

SAFER: So, you're absolutely, what, 100 percent positive it was not Lenell Geter who held up that restaurant?

MOONEY: Absolutely . . .

The next time any of us saw Lenell Geter he was our guest at the George Foster Peabody awards luncheon, free at last. No new trial. They just up and let him out of jail. Case dismissed.

I mention our winning the Peabody for this story because, like the Columbia DuPont, it is one of the few television awards worth mentioning. Most of them are a dime a dozen and are given as a way to get somebody to come and make a free speech. What they buy you is the dubious distinction of calling your show "award winning," a distinction that has become as overworked as "investigative journalism" and "in-depth reporting." If they weren't so overworked, I would use them to describe what Morley Safer and Suzanne St. Pierre did on the Geter story—another story that, admittedly, got a lot of newspaper coverage before we arrived on the scene. (That's not unusual. As I said earlier, we often follow up on newspaper stories, sometimes at the urging of a viewer, as in this case.) What Morley and Suzanne did was some good hard digging, and what they unearthed made a difference in getting Lenell Geter out of jail. Did it make *the* difference? Hard to say, but it's almost impossible to put something like that in a *60 Minutes* spotlight without something happening.

What do the people who sent Geter to jail say made the difference? They don't say. But it's very apparent that they wish they had never heard of Lenell Geter, Morley Safer or Suzanne St. Pierre.

THE BEAUTIFUL PEOPLE

One of the things you learn early on in New York is that the "beautiful people," for the most part, aren't all that beautiful. Cristina DeLorean is an exception. Marilyn and I had run into John and Cristina DeLorean here and there and had become somewhat friendly. We went to their house a couple of times and once they came to ours. That was about it, and that was before the cocaine bust that leap-frogged him from the pages of *Business Week* to the cover of *People.*

I knew Cristina better than I knew John, but I didn't know her all that well either. She and another one of New York's really "beautiful people," Christie Brinkley, worked on a television show I once owned. When the show failed to get off the ground, I sort of lost track of the DeLoreans. The next time I saw John he was in my living room in handcuffs—but that night he was in everybody's living room in handcuffs, as the star of the seven o'clock news.

It crossed my mind from time to time to do a *60 Minutes* story on the DeLoreans, but before John became star of the Evening News I had always nixed the idea. I just didn't think they were very compelling. Now they were—the tall, handsome American auto tycoon busted by the Feds and the dark, beautiful Italian wife who was standing by him. My God, it was right out of Harold Robbins!

A day or so after the bust I reached John at his mother-in-law's house in Los Angeles and told him we were interested in getting him on *60 Minutes.* He said he was eager to go on so he could tell the world how he had been set up in a scheme cooked up by Margaret Thatcher and Ronald Reagan. Thatcher's motive? According to John, to get back at him for the money the British government had invested in his car company and on which they had received no return. And Reagan's? According to John, a showcase trial to publicize the Administration's war on drugs.

"That's pure conjecture, John," I said. "I can't hang a story on that."

That's when he told me he had a tape recording of a London *Daily Mirror* editor on the phone to a forger in San Remo, bribing him to forge documents about DeLorean, ostensibly at the behest of the Thatcher government.

"Now you're talking," I told him.

He said he would call his attorney and have him release to me the tapes of that conversation between the *Daily Mirror* and the forger. The next day, DeLorean's attorney's secretary came around with the tapes.

I listened once, I listened twice. Then I read a written transcript of the conversations. Maybe I was dumb, but damned if I could find a smoking gun or even anything remotely resembling what DeLorean had told me was on the tapes.

I called Frank Cresci, the private investigator who had arranged to have the phone conversation taped. Cresci is one of those marvelous characters about whom you never really know very much. He is either the Consul of Monaco doubling as some sort of James Bond or some sort of James Bond doubling as the Consul of Monaco. I never knew which. Whatever he is, he is a charmer with an infectious laugh and my kind of sense of humor. Once when I called him for lunch he said he had to go to the OPEC meeting in Vienna.

"OPEC meeting?" I said. "What the hell is Monaco doing at an OPEC meeting?"

"If they cut back," he said, "if we don't get what we got last year, we're gonna have to close the gas station."

Anyway, I called Cresci to see what there was in the tape that I kept missing.

"Nothing," he said. "I kept trying to tell DeLorean there was nothing on the tape, but he didn't want to hear that."

What I heard and what was borne out by my conversation with Cresci was that far from trying to buy some forged documents, the *Daily Mirror* editor was insisting that the documents be genuine or he wasn't interested. That's when I learned to take anything I heard from DeLorean with a grain of salt. For instance, he told me it could be proved that he, John DeLorean, was one of the subjects on the agenda at the Versailles Summit Conference. When I asked him what evidence he had to document that, he said he couldn't document it but he was sure that if we started nosing around, we could come up with the documentation. All our conversations had that same unreal quality.

For months on end I wouldn't hear from him and then either John or Cristina or I would phone to resurrect the idea of one of them or both of them going on *60 Minutes*. John always said he'd do it only if we would put some top reporters on the job of investigating the Thatcher government. It got crazier and crazier. I finally figured the best thing to do was to write off getting DeLorean to talk with any candor.

Some months later, when DeLorean had exhausted his last chance for a delay, a date was set for his trial. I figured it couldn't do any harm to give it one more shot. I called Cristina at their estate in New Jersey and told her if the time had ever come it was now for John to go on *60 Minutes*. She asked me if we would present his side of the story. I told her no, that was his job not ours, but that an interview with Morley Safer would give him the chance to answer all the questions the American people were asking about him. "Okay," she said. "I'll call John in California and tell him I think he should go on *60 Minutes*."

A few minutes later John called from California and said, "Don, come on out. I'm ready."

I made arrangements to fly to Los Angeles the next day to meet with DeLorean and his attorney Howard Weitzman, but a funny thing happened on my way to DeLorean.

Joe Wershba stopped me in the hall and told me he had gotten a call from Larry Flynt, the publisher of *Hustler*, who said he had copies of the videotapes the government had made of DeLorean's meetings with drug dealers. "Call him," Wershba said. "Maybe he'll let you see them."

I called Flynt, told him I was coming to California to see DeLorean and asked if I could see him while I was there.

"Come to my house when you get here," he said. "I've got something interesting to show you."

The next afternoon when I arrived in Los Angeles I went directly to Flynt's house in Bel Air. It was, I was told, the old Errol Flynn place, and getting into the grounds was like getting into Fort Knox. There was a big locked gate tended by a uniformed guard armed with a pistol. He told me to use the phone that was in a box on the stone fence post and call inside to state my business. The last time I had done that was when Morley and I tried to get into Jean Peters' house to talk to her about her ex-husband Howard Hughes. That time I didn't get in. This time I did. The uniformed guard got a signal by walkie-talkie from inside the house to let the man at the gate pass. Once I was inside, another guard, wearing a holster on his belt, checked again to make sure the man they had let through the gate was really the man Flynt was expecting. Then I was taken to the door and met by another armed guard who told me to sit on a bench in the foyer outside Larry's office. I remarked to one of the guards who came through the foyer from time to time that I had never seen so much "iron" around a private citizen.

"Betcha ass," he said. "You couldn't get in here with a SWAT team."

Flynt had been shot several years before by a would-be assassin and was paranoid about his safety. I'm sure I would be too if someone had put a bullet in me and left me crippled and in a wheelchair.

Pretty soon the office door opened and a voice boomed out, "Don, come on in." There he was in his wheelchair, feisty, combative and raring to let the world know that he was down but not out.

Right off the bat he had a proposition. He told me that if we would run, uncut and in its entirety, a videotape he had made concerning the trial in Cincinnati in which he, as publisher of *Hustler* magazine, had been charged with pornography, he would give me the Vicki Morgan sex tapes, which he said showed Ronald Reagan, William French Smith, Bill Casey and other assorted members of the Reagan team in bed with Vicki Morgan, the late mistress of Reagan's pal Alfred Bloomingdale. "Come on, Larry," I said. "You're nuts." "Okay," he said. "Want to see some pictures of Congressman Larry MacDonald, the guy who was shot down in the Korean airliner over Russia?"

"Doing what?" I asked.

"Here," he said, and handed me a bunch of pictures of some guy in bed with a hooker. Whether it was MacDonald or not, I hadn't the slightest idea.

"You're making a mistake," Flynt said. Then he proceeded to tell me that Congressman MacDonald had been on his way to Korea to meet former CIA director Richard Helms and deliver to him copies of the Vicki Morgan sex tapes when Reagan got wind of the mission and arranged to have the plane shot down. I was beginning to think I had wandered into a nuthouse. Next, he told me that Jesse Helms, the Senator from North Carolina (no relation to the former CIA director), was conspiring to make "Henry Kissinger our first Nazi President."

"Larry, what the hell's the matter with you?" I said. "Kissinger's Jewish."

"That's what they want you to think," he said.

Now I knew I was in a nut house. I didn't have to wait for Joe Wershba to tell me that Larry had phoned him with the news that Jimmy Hoffa was alive in Manchuria and that Marilyn Monroe was living in Alaska—a story he later amended to "Hoffa is in Alaska with Marilyn Monroe but nothing is going on between them."

About this time I was beginning to suspect that the DeLorean tapes were in Alaska with Jimmy Hoffa and Marilyn Monroe or maybe in Korea with Richard Helms. But that's when Flynt surprised the hell out of me. He opened one of several attaché cases that were on the floor around his wheelchair and showed me a set of tapes labeled with the dates of the DeLorean drug meetings the FBI had recorded. Before showing them to me, he opened another briefcase and showed me $500,000 in cash. He said he kept it around the place to buy whatever he needed from God knows who—purveyors of dirty pictures, tellers of ridiculous stories or just plain sellers of information.

Larry asked me which of the DeLorean tapes I wanted to see first.

"The one where the feds move in and bust him," I told him. Sure enough, he showed it to me. In amongst all the cock-and-bull stories, I couldn't believe I was looking at the genuine article, but there it was on the screen.

"Can I borrow it, Larry, and have it copied?"

"Sure, why not?" he said.

"You want to send someone with me to make sure I bring it back?" I asked.

"Nah, I trust you."

Then he asked me if I wanted to hang around and meet the guy he got them from. I glanced at my watch. It was past six, so it was past nine in the East and the network would soon be shutting down for the night.

"Haven't got the time," I said. "I'll take them to the CBS newsroom, copy them and get them back to you later."

"Okay," he said.

So I never met the guy Flynt got the tapes from, although afterward he swore I did and is convinced I was the one who ratted on him to the FBI. In fact, he was so sure that I was the guy who blew the whistle on the guy who stole the tapes that he said at a news conference: "If Will Rogers never met a man he didn't like, it was because Will Rogers never met Don Hewitt."

An injunction by the trial judge to prevent us from airing the tapes was overturned the next Sunday afternoon by an appeals court, and that night they went on the air. Somehow, along the way, the fear that the showing of the tapes would make it impossible to get an impartial jury had disappeared. Not long after that a jury was picked and the trial began.

About the Vicki Morgan tapes. Flynt finally showed them to me one day when he was in New York. There was a guy made up to look like Ronald Reagan in bed with a girl made up to look like Vicki Morgan. Whoever she was, she wasn't much. Neither was he. Ronald Reagan never made it big in pictures, but I'm sure he would have been better in this part than the actor made up to look like him.

Oh yeah, did we ever get to interview DeLorean? No, that never happened, but it sure was fun pursuing him.

Why did Flynt give me the videotape? I don't know. Was it part of a conspiracy between DeLorean and Flynt to get the trial delayed? I don't know that either, but I have my suspicions. Why? Because there was a curious thread I kept coming across in the DeLorean story. First of all, after the tapes had aired, I learned from people around Larry Flynt that he had offered to give DeLorean money to tide him over during the trial and that he told DeLorean's attorney, Howard Weitzman, that if Cristina would come up to his house, he would hand her the dough. Remember, I had seen $500,000 in cash in one of Flynt's attaché cases. Subsequently, Cristina confirmed the story. So, the DeLorean-Flynt connection was a tighter one than I had suspected at the time.

Second, a guy who worked for Flynt told me there was a connection between DeLorean and the man who supposedly told DeLorean that his kids would be killed if he backed out of the drug deal. The same man was at DeLorean's house in New Jersey the night DeLorean first told the story about the threat to Aaron Latham of *Rolling Stone* magazine. Was the threat a cock-and-bull story cooked up by the two of them?

I put that to DeLorean one morning during a phone call in which he denied it and also denied that the guy worked for him but did admit he knew him. A few minutes later, Cristina called me and said she and John had discussed my theory about the threat in bed the night before and she just wanted to tell me I was wrong.

"What do you mean, Cristina," I said, "you discussed my theory in bed last night? I didn't mention it to John until this morning."

At that point, John, obviously listening on another extension, said, "Cristina, shut up!"

MORLEY SAFER:

From "The Cavalcade of Stars" came a cavalcade of Gleason characters—The Poor Soul, Reginald Van Gleason III, and a minor sketch about a Brooklyn couple named Kramden . . .

GLEASON:

Almost everybody was a Kramden in the neighborhood I lived in . . . When you think of him, the poor soul hasn't got a hell of a lot of ability, but he keeps trying . . . His schemes are all to make him and Alice happy and he fails and when he fails she feels a great deal of affection. She knows why he did it and he apologizes all the time . . . He's just an ordinary moxe trying to make it and just can't.

SAWYER
BRADLEY
REASONER
SAFER
WALLACE

I would have hired Diane Sawyer if her name were Tom Sawyer. I don't think anyone should get good marks or bad marks for being either a Tom or a Diane. Tough as it is to convince the women's magazines (who discovered her after I did), it was not as they insist—"time to put a woman on *60 Minutes.*" It was time to put Diane Sawyer on *60 Minutes.*

She says:

I thought they'd never ask.

In the spring of 1970, fresh from a local television station in Louisville, Kentucky, I came to New York and asked the Executive Producer of *60 Minutes* if I could join the broadcast. After all, I reasoned, I had covered everything from local fires to local fires. I had proven myself in the intellectual crucible of reading the local weather. I had sprayed my hair and memorized the record high and low temperatures in fifty states. *I was ready.* It would take nerve, as I saw it, for Hewitt to tell me no.

He found the nerve.

Time passed. I wound my way through several professional incarnations. I returned to CBS in 1978 with a sober sense of proportion. When the call came in 1981 to move to New York for the Morning News, I was happy. I loved the people there. I was even getting used to fighting with hookers and junkies for cabs at two-thirty in the morning. Then one day my assistant burst into my office with a bulletin. She had just heard Don tell a CBS seminar he hoped I would be able to join the *60 Minutes* team. He hadn't mentioned dates, but to me it seemed like the equivalent of reading in the parish notes that the Pope wants to name you a Cardinal. There are four inviolable institutions at CBS. The legacy of Edward R. Murrow. Walter Cronkite. Dan Rather. *60 Minutes.* I was pleased. I was honored. I was afraid it wasn't true.

By the time I arrived in San Francisco to cover the Democratic Convention in the summer of 1984, it had been widely rumored that I would be reassigned soon to *60 Minutes.* On the night before the opening of the Convention, Don and I both happened to be at an elegant dinner given by the Democratic National Committee Chairman Charles Manatt at the home of Gordon and Ann Getty. The talk of the party was that Walter Mondale apparently had decided to fire Manatt and replace him with Bert Lance. The politicians and journalistic heavies, all dressed in fancy clothes, were talking about little else except the Manatt-Lance affair, but in a sociable manner; after all, this was a dinner party.

The meal, beautifully cooked and exquisitely served, gets under way. Suddenly I feel a tug on my satin sleeve. It's Hewitt, crouched down behind me and whispering in my ear, "Hey, we've got a story here." He prods me to wipe the sauce off my lips and make some excuse to my table. Then we tiptoe through the candlelight and hanging plants over to Manatt's table. We ask him to step outside.

He's our host. He can't say no.

Once out in the hall, the two of us pepper him with questions like a couple of rookie wire-service reporters. Hey, is it true you're getting the ax? Whaddya think of Lance? The besieged man not only confirms the story but tosses in an acid quote or two.

Hewitt now commandeers a phone in the Getty library and calls a stunned overnight radio crew in New York. By this time, some of the other journalists at the party are starting to mill around the library, listening to the growing commotion and wondering what the hell Hewitt is up to. After all, this is not Sunday night at 7:00 P.M. He barks at them that this is our story. The superstars of journalism look perplexed and anxious. The next thing I know I'm on the air—live on radio, in satin and spangles, sharing our little scoop with the world, or whoever is listening to CBS Radio at about one-thirty in the morning, Eastern Daylight Time.

Diane was working so hard to impress me that she was the one for *60 Minutes* that she didn't notice I was working just as hard to impress her that *60 Minutes* was the one for her.

DIANE SAWYER:
Admiral Rickover, the controversial father of the nuclear submarine . . . hasn't given an unrestricted personal interview on television since 1957. At eighty-four, the admiral retains the famous style: combative, challenging, deliberately provocative.

RICKOVER:
I never have thought I was smart. I thought the people I dealt with were dumb. . . . I never read rules . . . never had a book of Navy regulations in my office. I prohibited it. One time some guy brought it in and I told him to get the hell out and burn it.

SAWYER:
But that's not working within the system.

RICKOVER:
My job was not to work within the system. My job was to get things done.

60 MINU
524 West
New York

DEAR *60 MINUTES* . . .

After our Helen Hayes story, we received maybe the nicest letter *60 Minutes* ever got. It came from Helen Hayes and it was written to Paul Loewenwarter, the producer on the story. It said: "No one, since Charles MacArthur in the early twenties, has changed my life as much as you and Mike Wallace have done with *60 Minutes.* People, friends and strangers alike, are treating me as something very special—even remarkable."

The late Charles MacArthur was, of course, married to Helen Hayes. Because it was MacArthur and the late Ben Hecht who had created my hero Hildy Johnson in their play *The Front Page,* I was even more thrilled when Mike showed me what Helen Hayes had scribbled at the bottom of her note to him: "P.S. I hope Charlie and Ben were tuned in."

That's my favorite letter. My favorite phone call was from a Colorado mayor who sued Dan Rather for $40 million and who, when the suit was thrown out of court, called and asked if he could at least have an autographed picture of Dan.

Not everyone who writes is a Helen Hayes, and some of the mail is unbelievable. There are those who tell us that anyone who votes for Reagan is a fascist, that everybody's phone is tapped, that the Joint Chiefs can't wait for World War III, and "you guys" have sold out to big business. On the other side, we get told we're "commie rats," which seems to mean people who favor school busing and oppose school prayer, worry about the environment and think Jane Fonda sometimes has a point. Mostly though, what we get is not hate mail but love letters with sensible, reasonable suggestions that we do something about this or that. I can't answer them all, but before turning them over to our audience service department, I look at a representative sampling of what people are saying. They come from all over and they tell me so much about America that when I've finished reading them and selecting which ones we're going to broadcast, I feel like I've been on the road with Charles Kuralt.

A FEW MINUTES WITH ANDY ROONEY

If Walter Cronkite is "Uncle Walter," then Andy Rooney is "Cousin Andy." While the rest of *60 Minutes* lives in posh offices with a view of the Hudson River and the sun setting over New Jersey, Andy works out of a windowless rabbit warren across the street. I think he's ashamed to be seen with us. Once a week he shuffles into my office like an itinerant peddler with a videotape under his arm and sort of dares me not to like it. If I suggest his piece could be shorter, he fixes me with a look that makes me feel he's about to write an essay about what a nerd I am. How would you like to be the subject of an Andy Rooney essay? I'd rather be interviewed by Mike Wallace. Rooney has threatened to quit more often than Wallace has threatened to slow down. I never believe either one of them but every couple of weeks I have the same conversation with Rooney.

"Please don't quit, Andy."

"I just don't want to be on *60 Minutes* anymore."

"I need you, Andy. Everybody loves you."

"You can find someone else."

"No, I can't, Andy. What do you really want?"

"I don't want anything."

"Yes, you do."

"Well, for one, I don't like being on every other week."

"Okay, you'll be on every week."

"And further, I don't like my pieces cut to under two minutes."

"Okay, we won't do that anymore, either."

"How 'bout two minutes and fifteen seconds?"

"Okay. Deal?"

"Yeah, but isn't the public getting tired of me? You don't need me anymore. You've got Wallace and Safer and Reasoner and Bradley and Sawyer."

"Come on, Andy, two minutes and fifteen seconds every week."

"Yeah, I guess so."

He's such a pain in the neck, but God help us, he's worth it.

PARTING SHOTS

So what makes a story a *60 Minutes* story? First of all, it has to tweak a responsive chord in an awful lot of people. When you tweak responsive chords, it's almost impossible not to get a rise out of somebody, like the woman who pointed her finger at me and said, "You people in television are responsible for John Hinckley shooting President Reagan."

"How so?" I said.

"Because he watched so much television."

"Okay, lady," I said, "how much television do you think John Wilkes Booth watched before he shot Lincoln, or Cain watched before he slew his brother Abel?" Did that convince her? I don't think so.

Viewers often think we are giving someone the *60 Minutes* stamp of approval just because we interview him. Viewers who were shocked at our interviewing South Africa's Prime Minister wrote and said: "Surely, you wouldn't have interviewed Adolf Hitler in the midst of the Holocaust." To which I replied: "Damned right we would." Despicable as he was, he was the biggest newsmaker of his time.

There were those who clucked their disapproval when we broadcast an interview with another statesman, Iran's Ayatollah Khomeini. He was the biggest newsmaker in the world right after his people took the U.S. Embassy hostage, and interviewing him at that time was more important than interviewing anyone else anywhere—good guy or bad guy. Mike was in California on a story when Barry Lando, one of our European producers, phoned New York and said that the Ayatollah had agreed to be interviewed. With Barry on one phone I got Mike on another and told him to hightail it to London—over the pole from Los Angeles. "There's one problem," Mike said. "I don't have my passport with me." I looked over at Mike's secretary, Mignette Hollyman, and said, "Ever been to London?" "Nope." "Got a passport?" "Yep." "Okay," I said, "you just won yourself a trip to England. Go to Mike's house, get his passport, get on the first plane to London and meet Mike at immigration when he lands. I'll arrange with Pan Am to get you to the gate where the plane arrives."

The meeting at the airport went off like clockwork. Then we began to sweat. The telephone service from the holy city of Qum, where Mike was going by car from Teheran to see Mr. Big, left a lot to be desired, so we just had to wait it out, wondering what would happen if the Ayatollah took a dislike to Mike and Barry. Suppose he had taken them prisoner along with the rest of the Americans he was holding? What then? Sunday morning we got word—I'm damned if I know how—that Mike and Barry and a camera crew had spent about an hour with the Ayatollah and were heading back to Teheran to feed the interview via the satellite. The next call came from Teheran. Mike and Barry were ready to feed.

The fact that Mike Wallace had seen Khomeini was by now on the wires, and just before the feed began I got a call from Hodding Carter, Assistant Secretary of State for Public Affairs, asking me if I could fill him in on what the Ayatollah had said.

After all, Mike was America's only contact with Khomeini. Hodding told me he had Secretary of State Cyrus Vance on another phone. I realized that filling him in before our broadcast violated every canon of good journalism, but to hell with it, I thought, this is different and maybe we can pass something on to Vance that might help get our guys out of there. "Hold on," I said, "the feed is about to begin and I'll give you a blow by blow account of what he told Mike." I don't know what value it was to Vance. It couldn't have been much, but it sure made me feel better to do it.

Mike was all pumped up when I got him on the phone later. He'd had very little sleep for days but getting a story like that one is what guys like Wallace live for. It's what fuels them.

"What was it like?" I asked him. "Lots of security?"

"Nah, one guy on a rooftop with a shotgun."

"Why didn't you kidnap him and swap him for the hostages?"

"Probably could have," Mike said.

"Mike," I said, "I had this crazy daydream that the son-of-a-bitch handed the hostages over to you and you brought them home."

"That's funny," said Mike. "The same thought crossed my mind, but I don't think those guys are coming home for a long time."

The next morning I read in the New York *Times*, which was refused an interview with Khomeini, that ours only served Iran's propaganda aims. I hit the ceiling. The same New York *Times* that day after day carried pictures of Iranian students waving placards castigating the United States had the nerve to point a finger at us. But, what the hell, I figure the New York *Times* has its share of muttonheads just like everyone else.

The problem is that a lot of newspaper people think television should be not a profit-making business like the one they're in, but a public utility accountable *not* to the public but to them. Just think how much more space newspapers could devote to real news if they didn't waste so much of it writing about us. The New York *Times*, the newspaper that boasts "All the news that's fit to print," has four times as many reporters assigned full time to television as it does to the United Nations. And hardly ever has one of these television reporters written as perceptively about television as their colleague Tom Wicker did after the TWA hijacking, when he reminded them: ". . . television has become the national nervous system"; and ". . . what most Americans knew of last year's presidential campaign was that they saw it on television"; and "how much reality would famine in Ethiopia have in Middletown, U.S.A., if it were not visible on the home screen?"

"Television," Wicker noted, "has become a condition of being. It may on occasion be inconvenient, intrusive, even harmful, but if because of government censorship or network self-censorship the hostage crisis had not been visible, *real*, on American screens, the outrage and outcry would have been one thousand times louder. . . and rightly so; for we depend on television for perception as we depend on air for breath. And that's the way it is."

So, when is somebody in the press, besides Tom Wicker, going to notice that when the public wants one kind of experience it picks up a newspaper; when it wants another kind it turns on television and really doesn't care what its favorite newspaper thinks of its favorite newscast or vice versa. That's also the way it is.

But if that's true, why do CBS News, NBC News and ABC News have press agents bombarding television columnists with publicity handouts? With all that free space available, they'd be fools not to. What do they expect to get out of it? The usual: "I don't care what you say about me, as long as you spell my name right."

About our being the national nervous system: It wasn't a role we sought, but something that was thrust on us in 1963 after that terrible day in Dallas. Anybody who thinks he's big enough to take it on is welcome to it.

I bitch a lot about print people telling me how to do my job, but it really hasn't caused me any anguish. It might have, if I had listened to them. If I had, today I'd probably be back at some version or other of Acme Newspictures scotch-taping captions to the bottom of black-and-white photos.

One of the things our critics harp on most are our outtakes. What we put in the trash seems to interest them as much as what we put on the air. We don't rummage around in their wastebaskets but they love to rummage around in ours.

There are outtakes and there are outtakes. The one I remember best is an outtake from a videotape we purchased of Frank Gannon, one of Nixon's former aides, interviewing the former President. We purchased the interview mostly because we had never before heard a former President so unguarded on the record. In viewing it, I was bowled over by Nixon's account of his first meeting (when Vice President) with Nikita Khrushchev. It was the most revealing thing I'd ever heard of what it's really like when world statesmen meet. According to Nixon, Khrushchev, in referring to a treaty the Senate had just passed, said to him, "That treaty stinks. It stinks worse that horseshit, and nothing stinks worse than horseshit." Nixon said he then told Khrushchev, "I beg to differ with you. Pig shit stinks worse than horseshit." "You may be right," the Premier of the USSR said to the Vice President of the U.S., "but that's the only thing you're right about."

Why didn't we use it? Wiser heads than mine prevailed. My boss, Ed Joyce, the president of CBS News, and Van Gordon Sauter, his boss, said that although it did bowl you over, it might be perceived that we had spent a lot of money only to do that—to bowl people over. They were right, and into the trash went my favorite outtake.

Have I made mistakes along the way? Sure, though never out of malice or deliberate disregard of the truth. The most glaring became a *cause célèbre* for Illinois Power and friends of theirs who do not like anything about *60 Minutes*. It came about when we made some mistakes in a November 1979 story about cost overruns at Illinois Power's Clinton, Illinois, nuclear plant, including not reporting that one of the critics of Illinois Power—a man we interviewed for the story—had falsified his credentials—and we knew it. Really inexcusable, but we tried to make restitution by reporting the facts on a later broadcast.

That didn't satisfy Illinois Power, which made and distributed throughout the country a very unflattering videotape about *60 Minutes* that is still being played for sympathetic audiences. That tape became the bible of the crowd that thinks *60 Minutes* is antibusiness and antinuclear. I've always thought that if Illinois Power had spent the same time, money and effort holding their own feet to the fire as they spent holding ours, their nuclear plant would have come in a lot closer to on time and a lot closer to on budget. About our role in this episode: if we hadn't been brushed back from the plate by Illinois Power's spitball and had stepped into the pitch instead of flinching, we would have hit one out of the park. In the story we did—the one they took us to task for—we said, and correctly, that the plant was two-and-a-half years behind schedule and a billion dollors over budget. Well, five years after Illinois Power took us over the coals for that story, the plant is now seven years behind schedule and more than two-and-a-half billion over budget. Have we reported that? I'm afraid not. You see, their beanball worked. (At least the new figures got into this book.)

Okay, what other ruckuses have we been involved in? There was, of course, the Galloway case, in which Dan Rather ended up on the witness stand testifying that we had done nothing improper in reporting about accident mills that "manufactured" auto accidents and clinics that fabricated medical reports as part of a scam. Dr. Galloway was related by marriage to a man who owned one of the clinics, and it was his name that had appeared on a fictitious medical report. He claimed that although it was his name, it wasn't his signature. We had made the reasonable assumption that if a doctor is the only doctor working at a clinic and his name is displayed on the wall, he is indeed the doctor who signs the clinic's reports. As Rather put it: "If it looks like a duck, walks like a duck and quacks like a duck, it's a duck." Galloway claimed his reputation had been damaged by his association with a phony clinic. A jury refused to award him a penny and acquitted us of any wrongdoing. Shortly after the verdict was rendered, a reporter arrived at my house and knocked on the door.

"Mr. Hewitt?" he said.

"Yes," I replied.

"May I talk to you about the Galloway case?"

"Sure," I said. "Come on in."

He asked me why we had said the signature was Galloway's without submitting it to a handwriting expert.

"You merely made the assumption that it was his signature?" he asked.

"True," I replied, "but not a bad assumption to make. Let me ask you something," I went on. "Are you going to publish this interview?"

"Sure am," he replied.

"Are you going to quote me?" I asked.

"Of course, I'm going to quote you," he said.

"Okay, Mr. Reporter," I said, "how do you know it's me?"

"What do you mean? How do I know it's you? I knocked on the door and said 'Mr. Hewitt?' and you replied 'yes.'"

"So you just made the assumption it was me," I said.

That did it. He left with his tail between his legs.

But all this begs the question: What about all those other lawsuits *60 Minutes* has been subjected to? The truth is, there have been thirty-seven of them and we have never lost one. Only one of them was settled out of court. That was a $5,000 payment to a relative of a man we said was a kingpin in the Bolivian narcotics trade. It was easier to pay him than go down there to fight it. P.S. He's never picked up the money.

About the Westmoreland trial: To this day, people are still confused about just where it was they saw the broadcast that gave rise to the trial. Because Mike Wallace was the reporter, a lot of people are sure they saw it on *60 Minutes.* They didn't. They saw it on a CBS News documentary called "The Uncounted Enemy."

Did the Westmoreland trial (which was not on *60 Minutes*) have what some people call "a chilling effect" on us? First of all, I have never heard anyone around here use the term "a chilling effect," so in that regard, no. But I'd be lying if I told you that the Galloway trial (which CBS won) and the Westmoreland trial (which CBS also won) had *no* effect. Closer to home than ever before was the realization that no matter how honest a reporter you are, there's always the possibility of being put through a wringer (as Dan Rather and Mike Wallace were) to prove to a jury that you are what you are and not what the opposing lawyer says you are.

Has the threat of having to defend ourselves in a lawsuit ever scared us off a story? No, never.

Just before I completed this book I was asked by Sigma Delta Chi, the journalism fraternity, to write a few words about freedom of the press. Here's what I sent them:

> Because we in America are blessed with the right to report fully and freely, it is incumbent on us to temper that right with restraint and good judgment.
>
> We have no right knowingly to do violence to the truth, whether we get caught or not. We have no right to distort. Most important of all, we must never forget we are not the only ones with rights and that there is such a thing as a right of privacy.
>
> That does not mean that citizens should be allowed to hide their malfeasances. What it does mean is that exercising our freedom to publish or broadcast should be in aid of something worthwhile.
>
> The best way to insure that we go on having the freedom to publish and broadcast is to guard against self-indulgence. Self-indulgence by the press is no more attractive or desirable than any other kind of self-indulgence.

Have I been involved in any self-indulgences? I'm afraid I have, and most of them are mentioned in this book.

Have I ever broken faith with our viewers? I think not, but I'm sure I could get an argument about that.

CREDITS

To anyone at *60 Minutes* who got left in the cutting room, no one knows better than you that something good always gets left in the cutting room. If this time it was you, I owe you one.

To Random House's Jason Epstein, in whose kitchen in Sag Harbor I was finally persuaded that he meant it when he said, "You oughta write a book," I owe you for a lot of things, not the least of which was putting me in the hands of an editor as good as Corona Machemer. I also owe one to my daughter Jillian, who helped with the selection of pictures for the book, along with Sallye Leventhal, Abid Ali, Bob Corujo, and Mike Durso, and to Beverly Morgan who helped with everything.

Writing the book was not as tough as I thought it would be, but then, nothing is when you have a spectacular wife like Marilyn and three wonderful kids like Jeffrey, Steven and Lisa.

GRAPHIC CREDITS

This book was photo-composed by University Graphics, Inc., Atlantic Highlands, New Jersey.
The text was printed and the book bound by Kingsport Press, Kingsport, Tennessee.
The color separations are by Beaumont Graphics, St. Louis, Missouri.
R.D. Scudellari designed and directed the graphics.
Naomi Osnos designed and coordinated the graphics.